Mastering Android Wear Application Development

Master the future of mobile devices in wearable technology

Siddique Hameed
Javeed Chida

BIRMINGHAM - MUMBAI

Mastering Android Wear Application Development

Copyright © 2016 Packt Publishing

First published: December 2016

Production reference: 1021216

Published by Packt Publishing Ltd.
Livery Place
35 Livery Street
Birmingham
B3 2PB, UK.
ISBN 978-1-78588-172-5

www.packtpub.com

Credits

Authors

Siddique Hameed
Javeed Chida

Copy Editors

Pranjali Chury
Safis Editing

Reviewers

Mark Elston

Project Coordinator

Suzanne Coutinho

Commissioning Editor

Edward Gordon

Proofreader

Safis Editing

Acquisition Editor

Sonali Vernekar

Indexer

Tejal Daruwale Soni

Content Development Editor

Zeeyan Pinheiro

Graphics

Kirk D'Penha

Technical Editor

Pavan Ramchandani

Production Coordinator

Shraddha Falebhai

About the Authors

Siddique Hameed is a pragmatic technologist currently working on Simplify Commerce (`https://simplify.com`), a payment gateway platform from MasterCard. During his diverse career roles, he's been crafting software for Fortune 500 companies to startups of industry domains ranging from finance, commerce, social media, telecom, bioinformatics, publishing, and insurance.

He is passionate about technology, software and their effects on day-to-day lives. He is a strong believer in open-source software culture and actively contributes to many open-source projects. On times, he speaks at technology events, meetups, and mentor contestants in hackathons. He likes teaching kids and adults in programming, technology and software development, and volunteers on coding initiatives such as *Girls Who Code, Code.org*, and STEM (science, technology, engineering, and mathematics) programs.

In his spare time, he likes traveling, goes on long road trips, and tinker with Raspberry Pi and build DIY gadgets.

Dedicated to my Mom, Dad, Wife, and two wonderful daughters!

Javeed Chida currently works as a senior software engineer for Apollo Education Group, a leader in global education. He has worked with several teams over the years developing multi-layered enterprise applications for companies spanning several industries including education, finance, medical, insurance, construction, and legal.

He is passionate about Java portals and particularly enthused by the Liferay portal platform. He also has a love for clever and innovative technical documentation. Apart from periodically churning out articles as a highlighted community blogger on `Liferay.com`. He spends his leisure absorbed in creative writing projects, particularly classical poetry and fiction.

About the Reviewer

Mark Elston is a software architect for an automated test equipment company working primarily in the IC and mobile device test world. However, his 30 years of experience includes developing aircraft and missile simulations for the Air Force and Navy, hardware control systems for NASA, and tester operating systems for commercial products. He has also developed several Android applications for fun. His latest passion is delving into the world of Functional Programming and Design.

I would like to thank my wife for her understanding when I had a chapter to finish reviewing. I would also like to thank Suzanne Coutinho for giving me the opportunity to work with her and the Packt team on this project. It has been enlightening and entertaining. Finally, I would like to thank the authors for taking even my smallest comments into account. It is a pleasure to be part of a project where your inputs are valued.

www.PacktPub.com

For support files and downloads related to your book, please visit www.PacktPub.com.

Did you know that Packt offers eBook versions of every book published, with PDF and ePub files available? You can upgrade to the eBook version at www.PacktPub.com and as a print book customer, you are entitled to a discount on the eBook copy. Get in touch with us at service@packtpub.com for more details.

At www.PacktPub.com, you can also read a collection of free technical articles, sign up for a range of free newsletters and receive exclusive discounts and offers on Packt books and eBooks.

https://www.packtpub.com/mapt

Get the most in-demand software skills with Mapt. Mapt gives you full access to all Packt books and video courses, as well as industry-leading tools to help you plan your personal development and advance your career.

Why subscribe?

- Fully searchable across every book published by Packt
- Copy and paste, print, and bookmark content
- On demand and accessible via a web browser

Table of Contents

Preface

This book is intended for developers working on mobile, desktop, or web platforms interested in learning how to build apps for wearable devices, also known as wear apps. Furthermore, you may already have apps featured on the Google Play store and are looking to provide Android Wear support for your existing Android apps. If either of these statements is true, then yes, this book is for you.

Our primary goal in this book is to provide you, the reader, with a solid understanding of the philosophy, thought process, development details, and methodologies involved in building well-designed and robust Android Wear applications. We'll cover the advantages and the disadvantages of the wearable computing paradigm, and in doing so, we hope to provide a strong foundation for building wearable apps to meet practical and real-world use cases.

We will explore a wide range of concepts and features, from basic to medium to advanced, with varying degrees of complexity. Code samples accompanying each chapter are intended to give you hands-on knowledge of using the tools, libraries, SDKs, and other relevant technology needed to build Android Wear apps.

As you journey through the chapters of this book, you can expect to achieve the following objectives:

- Understand wearable computing technology
- Set up your development environment for building Android Wear apps using Android Studio
- Begin a mastery of the Android Wear SDK and APIs
- Understand the commonly used UI patterns and UX principles surrounding Android Wear app development
- Work with different form factors of wearable devices (round, square)
- Take advantage of the sensors available on Android Wear devices
- Develop Android Wear sample apps to try out the concepts you learn
- Communicate between Android mobile (handheld) and Android Wear apps
- Learn how to publish Android Wear apps to the Google Play store

What this book covers

Chapter 1, *Introduction to Wearable Computing,* covers the basics of wearable computing in general and how the technology has evolved. It also includes discussions on mobile computing, ubiquitous computing, and cloud computing.

Chapter 2, *Setting up the Development Environment,* shifts the focus on getting the readers familiar with setting up a development environment, from IDE installation to a discussion of the SDKs and libraries needed for Android Wear development.

Chapter 3, *Developing an Android Wear App,* walks the reader through step-by-step instructions for developing an Android Wear application, the Today app, from scratch using Android Studio.

Chapter 4, *Developing Watch UIs,* extends the Today app using UI components available in the Android Wear SDK and builds custom UI components using custom layouts.

Chapter 5, *Synchronizing Data,* introduces the idea of the need for a companion handheld app, including the steps to pair a handheld with an Android Wear emulator, thereby expanding your environment for wearable app development. The Today app is further extended to demonstrate these concepts.

Chapter 6, *Contextual Notifications,* discusses notifications in Android Wear and extends the Today app with an On This Day activity to demonstrate the Android Wear Notifications API.

Chapter 7, *Voice Interactions, Sensors, and Tracking,* discusses the voice capabilities offered by the Wear API. We define a voice action to launch our app. We introduce device sensors and discuss how they can be used to track data.

Chapter 8, *Creating a Custom UI,* covers the design principles that are central to the Android Wear UI space and examines a few common Wear UI patterns. We also augment the On This Day activity to display in a user-friendly format.

Chapter 9, *Material Design,* provides a conceptual understanding of material design and touches upon a few key principles specific to wearable app design and development. We solidify our understanding by extending our Todo app from the previous chapters to incorporate a navigation drawer that lets us switch between to-do categories, view items, and perform actions specific to each category.

Chapter 10, *Watch Faces,* introduces the concept of watch faces in this chapter. After a brief survey of the Android Wear APIs available to help us develop watch faces, we develop a simple interactive watch face.

`Chapter 11`, *Advanced Features and Concepts*, describes the design concerns and API features related to making apps run as if they were always on. We develop an activity to demonstrate the always-on capability provided by the Wear API. We also touch upon debugging wear apps over Bluetooth connections.

`Chapter 12`, *Publishing Apps to Google Play*, discusses the tooling available to test Android Wear apps and how to automate UI testing. We conclude the chapter with step-by-step instructions to get the app ready for publishing.

What you need for this book

You will require the following set of tools to try out the codes in the book and to practice the application development yourself:

- Android Studio v2 or greater
- JDK v7 or greater
- Git version control
- A development system with decent hardware configurations, such as a fast CPU and adequate RAM for developing mobile applications

Who this book is for

Java application developers--web, desktop, or mobile who wants to gain exposure to the Android Wear platform and equip themselves with the knowledge necessary to master the development of Android Wear apps.

Conventions

In this book, you will find a number of text styles that distinguish between different kinds of information. Here are some examples of these styles and an explanation of their meaning.

Code words in text, database table names, folder names, filenames, file extensions, path names, dummy URLs, user input and Twitter handles are shown as follows: "We can include other contexts through the use of the `include` directive."

A block of code is set as follows:

```
public static void Main(string[] args)
{
var host = new WebHostBuilder()
.UseKestrel()
}
```

Any command-line input or output is written as follows:

```
vi run json
```

New terms and important words are shown in bold. Words that you see on the screen, for example, in menus or dialog boxes, appear in the text like this: "Clicking the **Next** button moves you to the next screen."

Warnings or important notes appear in a box like this.

Tips and tricks appear like this.

Reader feedback

Feedback from our readers is always welcome. Let us know what you think about this book—what you liked or disliked. Reader feedback is important to us as it helps us develop titles that you will really get the most out of. To send us general feedback, simply e-mail feedback@packtpub.com, and mention the book's title in the subject of your message. If there is a topic that you have expertise in and you are interested in either writing or contributing to a book, see our author guide at www.packtpub.com/authors.

Customer support

Now that you are the proud owner of a Packt book, we have a number of things to help you to get the most from your purchase.

Downloading the example code

You can download the example code files for this book from your account at http://www.packtpub.com. If you purchased this book elsewhere, you can visit http://www.packtpub.com/support and register to have the files e-mailed directly to you.

You can download the code files by following these steps:

1. Log in or register to our website using your e-mail address and password.
2. Hover the mouse pointer on the SUPPORT tab at the top.
3. Click on Code Downloads & Errata.
4. Enter the name of the book in the Search box.
5. Select the book for which you're looking to download the code files.
6. Choose from the drop-down menu where you purchased this book from.
7. Click on Code Download.

Once the file is downloaded, please make sure that you unzip or extract the folder using the latest version of:

- WinRAR / 7-Zip for Windows
- Zipeg / iZip / UnRarX for Mac
- 7-Zip / PeaZip for Linux

The code bundle for the book is also hosted on GitHub at https://github.com/PacktPublishing/Mastering-Android-Wear-Application-Development. We also have other code bundles from our rich catalog of books and videos available at https://github.com/PacktPublishing/. Check them out!

Downloading the color images of this book

We also provide you with a PDF file that has color images of the screenshots/diagrams used in this book. The color images will help you better understand the changes in the output. You can download this file from https://www.packtpub.com/sites/default/files/downloads/MasteringAndroidWearApplicationDevelopment_ColorImages.pdf.

Errata

Although we have taken every care to ensure the accuracy of our content, mistakes do happen. If you find a mistake in one of our books—maybe a mistake in the text or the code—we would be grateful if you could report this to us. By doing so, you can save other readers from frustration and help us improve subsequent versions of this book. If you find any errata, please report them by visiting http://www.packtpub.com/submit-errata, selecting your book, clicking on the Errata Submission Form link, and entering the details of your errata. Once your errata are verified, your submission will be accepted and the errata will be uploaded to our website or added to any list of existing errata under the Errata section of that title.

To view the previously submitted errata, go to https://www.packtpub.ccm/books/content/support and enter the name of the book in the search field. The required information will appear under the Errata section.

Piracy

Piracy of copyrighted material on the Internet is an ongoing problem across all media. At Packt, we take the protection of our copyright and licenses very seriously. If you come across any illegal copies of our works in any form on the Internet, please provide us with the location address or website name immediately so that we can pursue a remedy.

Please contact us at copyright@packtpub.com with a link to the suspected pirated material.

We appreciate your help in protecting our authors and our ability to bring you valuable content.

Questions

If you have a problem with any aspect of this book, you can contact us at questions@packtpub.com, and we will do our best to address the problem.

1
Introduction to Wearable Computing

"The more you know about the past, the better prepared you are for the future."

– Theodore Roosevelt

In this chapter, we will discuss the evolution of wearable computing and understand how it fits with other computing paradigms, such as desktop, mobile, and ubiquitous computing.

Evolution

Wearable computing, although widely believed to be the latest technological innovation, had existed even during the days of the abacus, a calculating tool that was used centuries ago by merchants and traders. According to a historical source on Chinese culture, it is believed that an abacus inlaid in a ring was used as a calculator during the *Qing dynasty* (`http://www.chinaculture.org/classics/2010-04/20/content_383263_4.htm`):

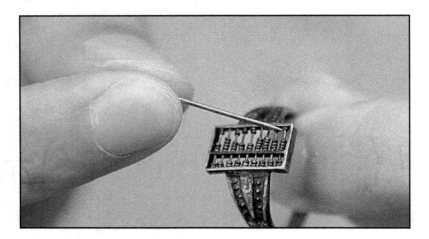

A relatively recent modern form of wearable computing devices is the Casio Databank. It's a series of electronic wristwatches manufactured by Casio during the early 1980s that were bundled with features such as a calculator, timer, world clock, contact management, and also a remote control for TV and VCR.

It was very popular and was considered a technological marvel of that time. It was very convenient compared to the manual or simple digital watches that were available during that time. It was not only used for checking the time and setting up alarms but also helped with utility functions such as calculating something fast on the fly or for recalling stored contact information:

Innovators and inventors have always been fascinated with bringing technology and lifestyle as close together as possible. Whether it's the Burton Amp jacket, which is believed to the first known modern wearable device for controlling iPods, or the latest wearable device called **Whistle** that is used by pet owners for tracking their pet's location and activity, wearable devices are becoming commonplaces.

Moore's law

Gordon Moore, co-founder of Intel, predicted 50 years ago that the number of transistors fitted into smaller integrated circuits would be doubled approximately every two years. That was the baseline for the explosive growth of computing powers. The size of the electronic components slowly became smaller and the processing power of the devices got stronger as time went by.

The mainframe computers, used in the early 1960s and 1970s to run enterprises and large corporations, occupied the size of a living room. They subsequently shrunk to mid-range servers and desktop computers. Integrated circuit chips and microprocessors used in computers got more and more powerful, the size of the storage devices got much smaller, and the size of the storage capacity got increased.

Desktop computers slowly transformed to become more portable in the form of laptops and notebook computers. Laptop computers are equipped with a rechargeable battery that can let users work on their computers for their personal or business needs whenever and wherever they wanted.

The **Personal Digital Assistant (PDA)** is used as the mobile computing device for managing contacts and performing some basic business-related tasks.

Then came the era of smartphones. When Steve Jobs introduced the iPhone in 2007, there were some smartphones already available on the market. However, the introduction of iPhones by Apple and the subsequent launch of the Android platform by Google led the way to strong and healthy competition in the smartphone industry.

What we are seeing now in the wearable devices trend is history repeating itself. But this time, Google took an early lead in launching the Android Wear platform in 2014, whereas Apple announced its first wearable watch in April 2015.

Major companies such as Samsung, LG, Pebble, and Jawbone have all jumped onto this bandwagon with varieties of wearable device available on the market already.

Ubiquitous computing

Ubiquitous computing is a computing paradigm where the human interaction with a computer happens anywhere and everywhere and through any device around them. Let's say, for example, that you are working on an important business proposal using your office desktop computer and you are almost done with your proposal document, but it's time to leave the office and pick up your kid from school and take her to swimming practice. You left work, picked up your kid, and took her to the swimming school. While she is doing her swimming practice, you continue to work on the business proposal from where you left off using your smartphone and send the document to the client just before she is done with the swimming practice.

While you are driving home, you get a response e-mail from the client. The computer integrated into the car you are driving is equipped with an app or system like *Siri* or *Alexa* that reads the e-mail message you received from the client out loud. And when you reach home, you respond to the client's business proposal using your smartwatch and even set up a date and place for the next meeting.

This example might sound a little exaggerated, but the important point to make here is that it's not the technology taking over human lives, it's the humans doing what they want to do whenever and wherever, seamlessly, and using simple interactions. The devices around them would help them do what they want to do without knowing or feeling that they do. That is the foundation philosophy of ubiquitous computing. It just lets you do things wherever you need to without asking or needing to know if that can be done there.

Human interaction with a computing device can be pervasive and it can happen without even knowing that it happens.

Technologies such as cloud computing and wireless communication protocols and standards such as Bluetooth, **Bluetooth Low Energy** (**BLE**), **Near Field Communications** (**NFC**), **Radio Frequency Identifications** (**RFID**), and ZigBee make such interactions with devices possible by forming the infrastructure needed for all these devices to communicate with each other and build the contexts needed.

Application developers, designers, and service providers should design their apps and services so that the users may interact with them anywhere and using any devices around them. Every device has its own form factor and is built for certain needs. Understanding the user context and the need for interaction with the device is very important when building apps that will provide great user experience. For instance, it may not be practical to have a keyboard-like UI component in a watch app due to its size and form factor, whereas it may be feasible to use voice input using a text-to-speech feature provided within wearable platforms.

Mobile meets wearables

Smartphones have become an integral part of our day-to-day life over the last decade or so. They have become a natural extension of ourselves and have made us carry them everywhere in our pockets, handbags, or purses to help us fulfill our day-to-day tasks. They are used to perform mundane to more important tasks. The tasks that were performed using personal computers or laptops have slowly been done through pocket-sized smartphones or tablets.

The reason smartphones have reached a high level of adoption and popularity is due to their portability. They are light relative to personal laptops, easy to carry around, and users can use them pretty much anywhere they are needed.

Although mobile phones and tablets can satisfy most computing needs on the go, they're not very convenient in many situations. Mobile phones are not easy when you are already busy with one hand and want to work with the phone in the other hand. To do subtle tasks such as checking the current time or have a quick look at incoming text notifications, you still need to remove the phone from the pocket or remove it from the purse. Wearable devices can help us get things done faster with simpler and quicker interactions.

Wearable computing is the next big frontier in computing innovation. It has all kinds of possibilities and advantages. Although the smartphones are considered *very personal devices*, they are not quite as intimate as wearable devices such as smartwatches or fitness activity trackers. Wearable devices or body-borne devices have the advantage of being on the body all the time and measuring important metrics such as heart rate, walk steps, and body temperature.

They have a huge potential in the healthcare market, where they can monitor our health condition every minute and guide users through the steps needed to have a healthy lifestyle.

Wearable devices can also be used for biometric authentication. There are some startups, such as **Nymi** (https://www.nymi.com/the-nymi-band/), who use individual heart and pulse rates as an identification factor for authentications.

How about we stop carrying the RFID-based access cards for entering buildings and use a wearable watch for authentication? It may even stop us needing to remember all kinds of passwords for various online websites; instead, we could use biometric data such as heart rate and iris recognition and build an authentication profile for logging into those systems.

Hello Android Wear

Android Wear is Google's port of the Android operating system designed for wearable devices such as smartwatches. At the time of writing, there are over a dozen manufacturers, such as LG, Motorola, Huawei, Asus, Fossil, and TAG Heuer, who make Android Wear watches:

The primary difference between the Android Wear platform and its competitor Apple's **watchOS** platform is the support of devices and screen sizes.

Unlike Apple Watch, which is currently available only in 42 mm and 38 mm rectangular screen sizes, Android Wear comes in the round, square, and rectangular screen shapes. They also come in various different screen sizes other than the standard 42 mm and 38 mm sizes.

Another key thing to note is that Android Wear devices can be paired using Android Wear apps for both Android and iOS platforms.

In this book, we'll be covering the topics involved in Android Wear application development and helping you master the platform for writing rich and powerful Android Wear applications.

Summary

In this chapter, we discussed the wearable computing paradigm and contrasted it with the mobile and desktop computing platforms.

In the next chapter, we'll be diving into topics related to setting up the environment for Android Wear application development using Android Studio IDE. So, buckle up and get ready for the fun and exciting ride ahead.

2
Setting up the Development Environment

"Give me six hours to chop down a tree and I will spend the first four sharpening the axe."
– Abraham Lincoln

In this chapter, we will discuss the steps, topics, and process involved in setting up a development environment using the Android Studio. If you have done Android application development using Android Studio, some of the items discussed here might already be familiar to you. However, there are some Android Wear platform-specific items that may be of interest to you.

Android Studio

Android Studio **Integrated Development Environment (IDE)** is based on the **IntelliJ IDEA** platform. If you have done Java development using IntelliJ IDEA platform, you'll feel at home working with Android Studio IDE.

Android Studio platform comes bundled with all the necessary tools and libraries needed for Android application development. If this is the first time you are setting up Android Studio on your development system, make sure that you have satisfied all the requirements before installation. Refer to the Android developer site (`http://developer.android.com/sdk/index.html#Requirements`) to check the items needed for the operating system of your choice.

Note that you need at least JDK version 7 installed on your machine for Android Studio to work. You can verify your JDK version by typing the following commands in the Terminal window:

```
SiddiquesMBP:~/Projects$ java -version
java version "1.7.0_55"
Java(TM) SE Runtime Environment (build 1.7.0_55-b13)
Java HotSpot(TM) 64-Bit Server VM (build 24.55-b03, mixed mode)
SiddiquesMBP:~/Projects$ javac -version
javac 1.7.0_55
```

If your system does not meet that requirement, upgrade it using the method that is specific to your operating system.

Installation

The Android Studio platform includes Android Studio IDE, SDK Tools, Google API Libraries, and system images needed for Android application development:

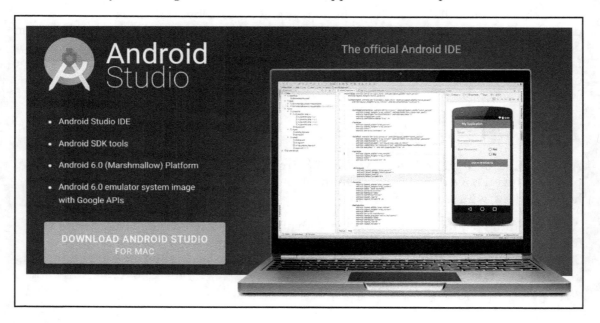

Visit the `http://developer.android.com/sdk/index.html` page to download Android Studio for your corresponding operating system and follow the installation instructions.

Git and GitHub

Git is a distributed version control system that is used widely for open source projects. We'll be using Git for sample code and sample projects as we go along the way.

Make sure that you have Git installed on your system by typing the following command in a Terminal window:

```
SiddiquesMBP:~/Projects$ git --version
git version 2.5.4 (Apple Git-61)
SiddiquesMBP:~/Projects$
```

If you don't have it installed, download and install it by visiting, `https://git-scm.com/do wnloads`link for your corresponding operating system.

If you are working on Mac OS El Capitan or Yosemite, or Linux distributions such as Ubuntu, Kubuntu, or Mint, the chances are you already have Git installed.

GitHub (`http://github.com`) is a free and popular hosting service for Git-based open source projects. They make checking out and contributing to open source projects easier than ever. Sign up with GitHub for a free account if you don't have an account already.

We'll be using GitHub to check out various sample projects related to Android Wear and also for sample code for applications developed for this book. We don't need to be an expert on Git for Android application development, but we do need to be familiar with the basic usage of Git commands to work with the project.

Android Studio comes by default with Git and GitHub integration. It helps to import sample code from Google's GitHub repository and helps you learn by checking out various application code samples.

Gradle

Android application development uses Gradle (`http://gradle.org/`) as the build system. It is used to build, test, run, and package the apps for running and testing Android applications.

Gradle is declarative and uses *convention over configuration* for build settings and configurations. It manages all the library dependencies for compiling and building code artifacts.

Fortunately, Android Studio abstracts most of the common Gradle tasks and operations needed for development. However, there may be some cases where having some extra knowledge about Gradle would be very helpful. We won't be digging into Gradle now, we'll be discussing it as and when needed during the course of our journey.

Android SDK packages

When you install Android Studio, it doesn't include all the Android SDK packages that are needed for development. The Android SDK separates tools, platforms, and other components and libraries into packages that can be downloaded, as needed using the Android SDK Manager. Before we start creating an application, we need to add some required packages into the Android SDK.

Launch SDK Manager from Android Studio, **Tools** | **Android** | **SDK Manager**:

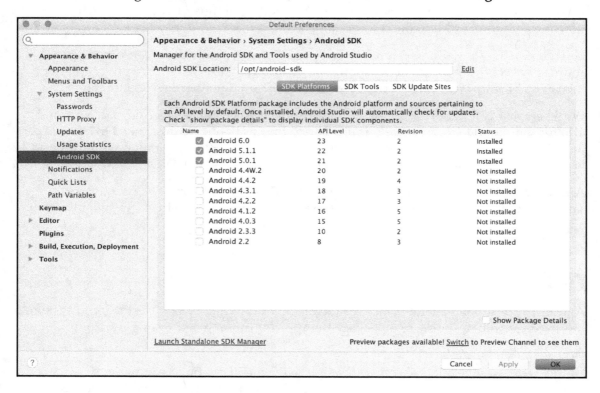

Let's quickly go over a few items in the preceding screenshot.

As you can see, the Android SDK's location is `/opt/android-sdk` on my machine. It may very well be different on your machine depending on what you selected during the Android Studio installation. The important point to note is that the Android SDK is installed in a different location than Android Studio's path (`/Applications/Android\ Studio.app/`).

This is considered a good practice because the Android SDK installation can be unaffected depending on a new installation or upgrade of Android Studio or vice versa.

On the **SDK Platforms** tab, select some recent Android SDK versions such as Android versions 6.0, 5.1.1, and 5.0.1.

Depending on the Android versions you are planning on supporting in your wearable apps, you can select other older Android versions.

Checking the **Show Package Details** option in the bottom right will show all the packages that will be installed for a given Android SDK version:

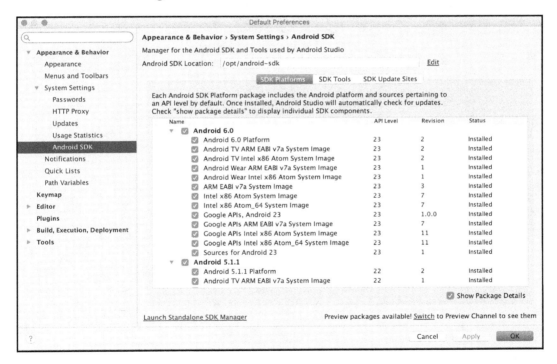

To be on the safe side, select all the packages. As you may have noticed already, Android Wear ARM and Intel system images are included in the package selection.

Now, when you click on the **SDK Tools** tab, make sure the following items are selected:

- **Android SDK Build Tools**
- **Android SDK Tools 24.4.1** (latest version)
- **Android SDK Platform-Tools**
- **Android Support Repository, rev 25** (latest version)
- **Android Support Library, rev 23.1.1** (latest version)
- **Google Play services, rev 29** (latest version)
- **Google Repository, rev 24** (latest version)
- **Intel X86 Emulator Accelerator (HAXM installer), rev 6.0.1** (latest version)
- **Documentation for Android SDK** (optional)

The SDK window will look like the following:

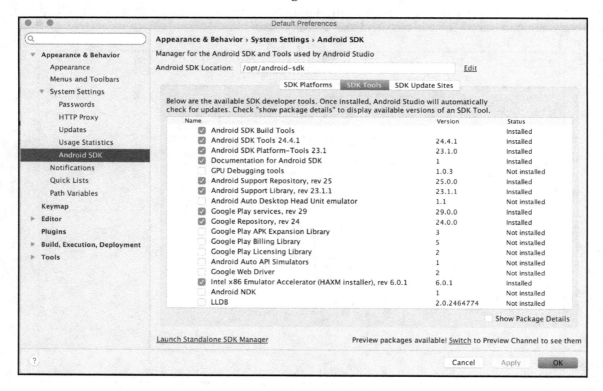

Do not change anything in the **SDK Update Sites** tab. Keep the update sites as it was configured by default.

Click on **OK** button. It will take some time to download and install all the components and packages selected.

Android Virtual Devices

Android Virtual Devices (AVD) will enable us to test the code using Android emulators. It lets us pick and choose various Android system target versions and form factors needed for testing.

Launch Android Virtual Device manager from **Tools** | **Android** | **AVD Manager**.

From the **AVD Manager** window, click on the **Create New Virtual Device** button in the bottom left and proceed to the next screen and select the **Wear** category:

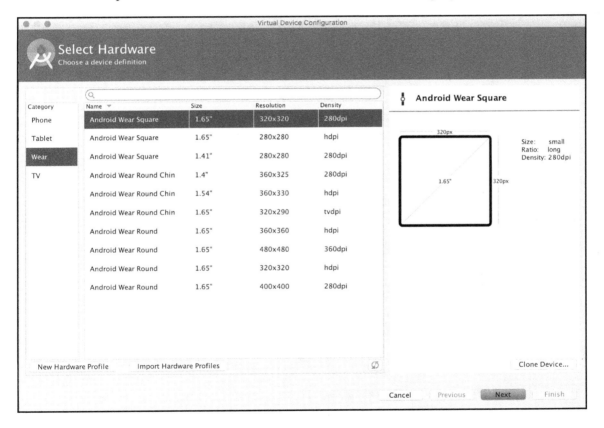

Select **Marshmallow** API Level **23 on x86** and leave everything else as the default settings, as shown in the following screenshot:

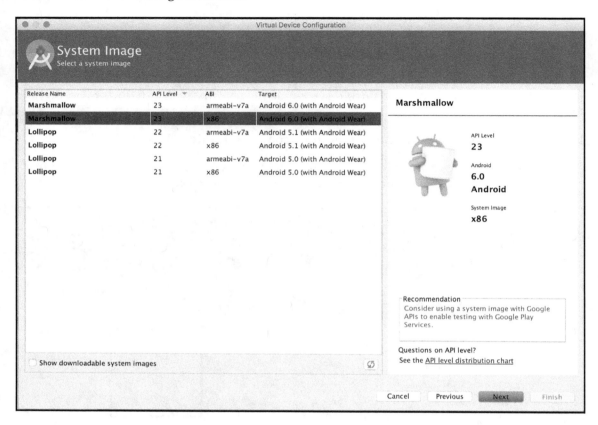

 Note that the current latest Android version is Marshmallow of API level 23 at the time of writing. It may or may not be the latest version while you are reading this chapter. Feel free to select the latest version that is available during that time. Also, if you'd like to support or test in earlier Android versions, feel free to do so on that screen.

The configuration window will appear after clicking the **Next** button:

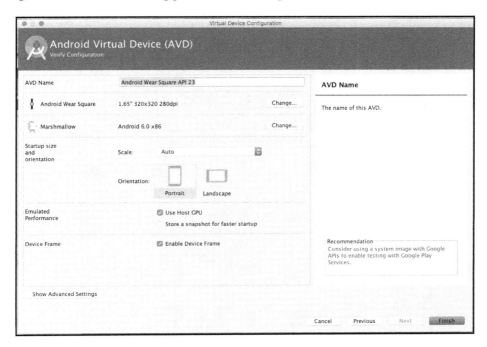

After the virtual device is selected successfully, you should see that listed on the **Android Virtual Devices** list, as shown in the following screenshot:

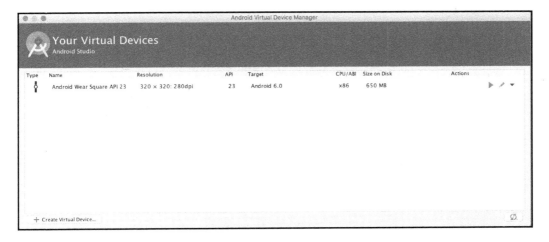

Although it's not a requirement to use real Android Wear device during development, sometimes it may be convenient and faster developing it in a real physical device. But for the sake of this book, we'll be primarily covering developing and testing using Android emulators.

Let's build a skeleton application

Since we have all the components and configurations needed for building a wearable app, let's build a skeleton app and test out what we have so far.

From Android Studio's **Quick Start** menu, click on the **Import an Android code sample** option:

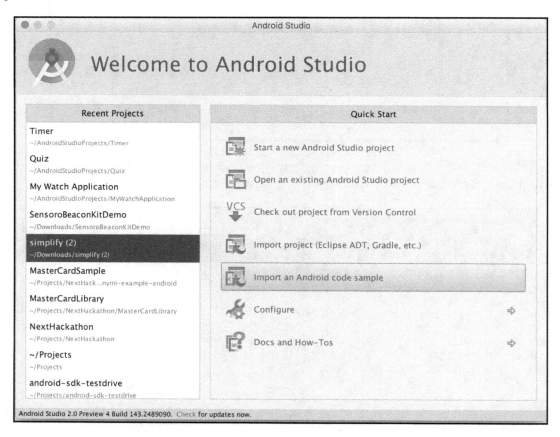

Select **Skeleton Wearable App** from the **Wearable** category:

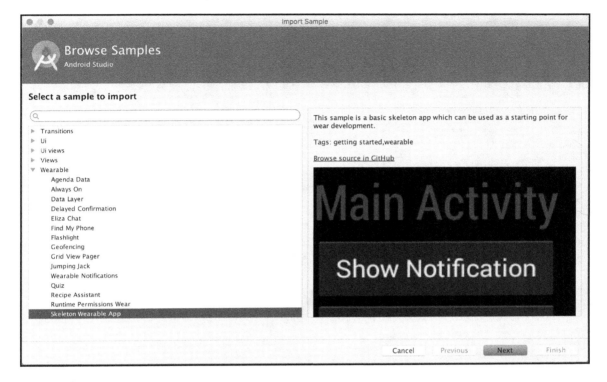

Click **Next** and select your preferred project location.

As you can see, the skeleton project is cloned from Google's sample code repository from GitHub:

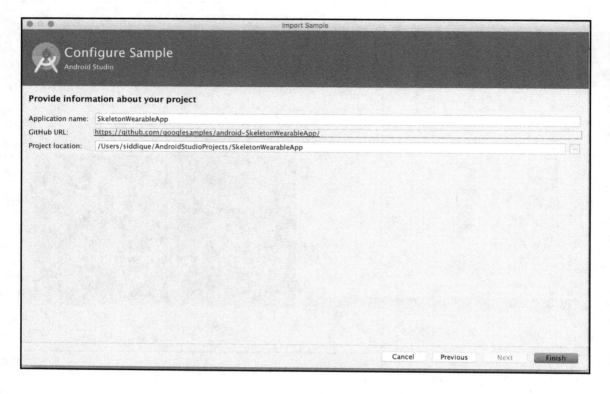

Clicking on the **Finish** button will pull the source code, and Android Studio will compile and build the code and get it ready for execution.

The following screenshot indicates that the Gradle build has finished successfully without any errors. Click on the green play button as shown in the following screenshot to run the configuration:

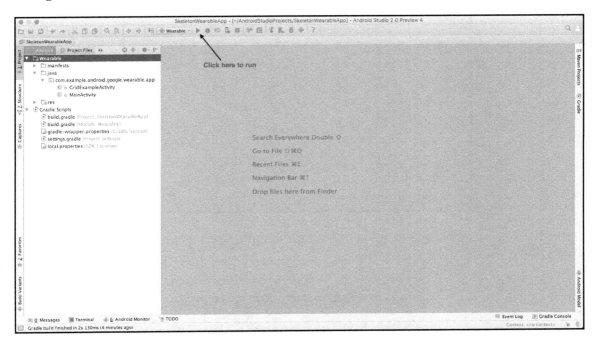

When the app starts running, Android Studio will prompt us to select the deployment targets. We can select the emulator we created earlier and click **OK**:

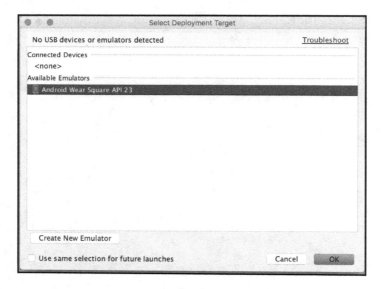

After the code compiles and is uploaded to the emulator, the main activity of the Skeleton App will be launched as shown here:

Clicking on the **SHOW NOTIFICATION** tab will show the notification:

Clicking on **START TIMER** tab will start the timer and run it for 5 seconds, and clicking on **FINISH ACTIVITY** will close the activity and take the emulator to the home screen:

Summary

We discussed the process involved in setting up the Android Studio development environment by covering the installation instructions, requirements, SDK tools, packages, and other components needed for Android Wear development.

We also checked out the source code for a skeleton wearable app from Google's sample code repository and successfully ran and tested it on the Android device emulator.

In the next chapter, we'll be working on a real-world Android Wear application from scratch with all the configuration and setup we have created so far.

3
Developing Android Wear Applications

"All compromise is based on give and take, but there can be no give and take on fundamentals. Any compromise on mere fundamentals is a surrender. For it is all give and no take."

- Mahatma Gandhi

In this chapter, we will be covering the concepts involved in the sample skeleton project that we imported using Android Studio in the previous chapter. We will be discussing the code involved in detail to help us gain some understanding of the fundamental building blocks of an Android Wear application.

Then, we'll be creating a new Android Wear app from scratch using Android Studio. We'll walk through the steps involved in creating the app and discuss the code changes needed and run the app to see the desired outcome.

Let's roll up our sleeves and see some code in action.

Skeleton app

If you recall from the previous chapter, we used Android Studio to import the sample project to build a skeleton wearable application. If you wonder where we got all the code from, here is the GitHub repository link for that project, `https://github.com/googlesampl es/android-SkeletonWearableApp/`.

Android Studio gets updated all the time. At the time of writing, Android Studio 2.0 preview 7 is the latest version currently available. It may or may not be the same version while you are reading this book.

If, for some reason, Android Studio doesn't let you import the Skeleton wearable app or the repository of the sample code is not available in Google's Samples GitHub repository, you can clone it from the fork I created for that project in my GitHub repository, `https://github.com/siddii/android-SkeletonWearableApp`.

> If you have done any Android app development before, you'll be able to follow this chapter. If not, this is a good time to brush up on some Android application development basic concepts and foundations.

The Android manifest file

Every Android application consists of an Android manifest file named `AndroidManifest.xml`. It contains all the essential information needed for the Android operating system to launch the application. The manifest file is used for declaring the activities, services, intents, SDK versions, features, permissions, and other application-specific components and behavioral elements for the Android application.

We should pay close attention to line number 23 of the Android manifest file that was included in the Skeleton wearable app:

```
<uses-feature android:name="android.hardware.type.watch" />
```

This line basically explains to the Android operating system that it is an Android Wear app. To prove this out, let's try commenting out this line from the `AndroidManifest.xml` file and launch the application. You should see the following error message when you launch the application using an emulator:

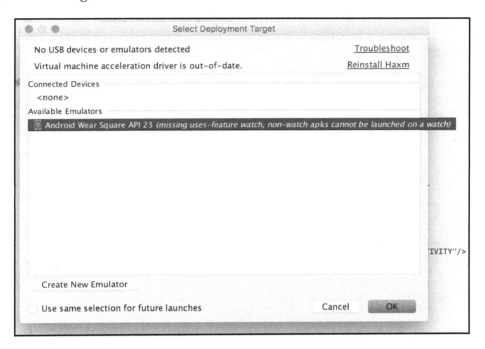

Gradle build files

Let's take a look at how the Gradle build files are configured. The settings.gradle file in the root folder includes all the modules for this project. In this case, it's just one module, which is the Wearable module folder:

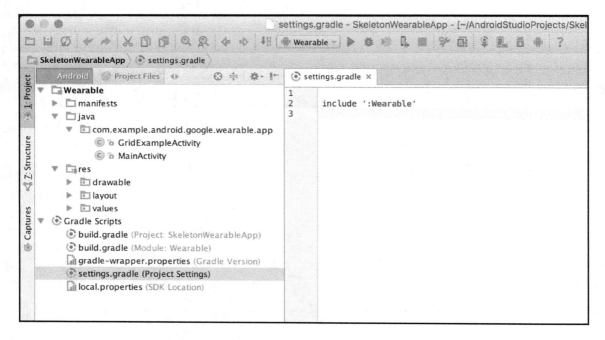

You will notice that there are two build.gradle files. One is at the project level and the other is inside the Wearable folder's module level.

The project's build.gradle file is empty because we don't have anything specific to the project build settings, whereas the build.gradle file in the Wearable module contains all the build configurations for this app:

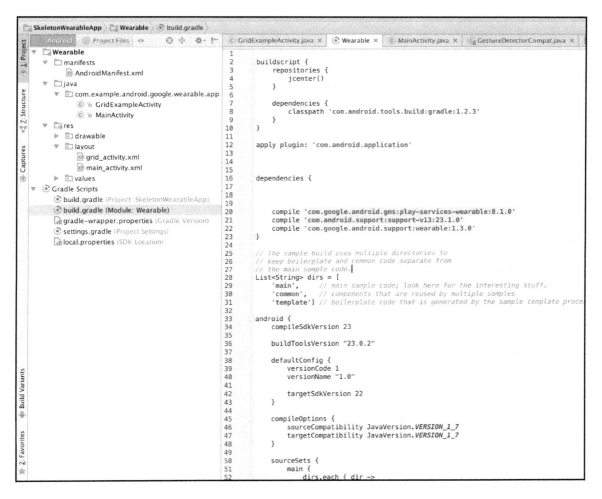

Lines 20, 21, and 22 of the `build.gradle` file specifies the external build dependencies for this project. Line 20 includes the dependency for **Google Play Services**, which is an integral part of the Android Wear platform. Google Play Services is used heavily for data synchronization and communication between the Android phones and wearable devices. We'll be covering them in detail in later chapters.

Line 21 includes the dependency for the `v13` support library. The reason is that we use **Fragment** inside the `GridExampleActivity` class.

Obviously, line 22 includes the dependency for the wearable support library since it's a wearable application.

The rest of the configuration is pretty standard for Android applications, including the source path, compile and target SDK versions, and the app's version settings.

App activities

The skeleton project consists of two activities, `MainActivity` and `GridExampleActivity`. The `MainActivity` activity contains a header text with `Main Activity` and three buttons inside `ScrollView` layout.

Let's take a look at the `main_activity.xml` file to see how the component layout is structured. One of the biggest advantages to developing Android applications using Android Studio is its layout editor. Although it may not be precisely the same during runtime, it can give a closer idea in terms of how the UI components are rendered during runtime.

After you have opened the `main_activity.xml` file, make sure you have the **Preview** tool window selected on the right side of Android Studio:

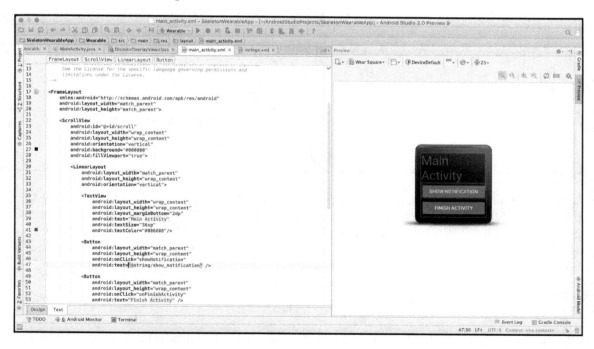

The Android Studio layout editor will display the live preview for changes to layout files. It also helps to get an understanding of how the components will be laid out for different form factors. As we know, Android Wear comes in square and circle-shaped form factors, so it will be a good idea to check how the components are laid out in both square and circle forms.

Clicking on the layout drop-down menu will display all the form factors available in the SDK and tool configurations:

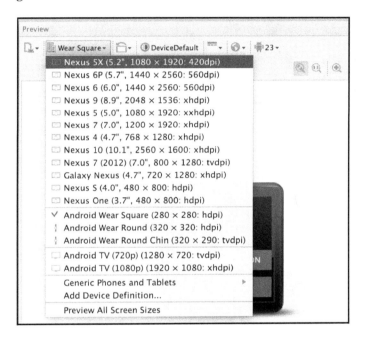

If you select the **Android Wear Round** layout, then you'll be able to see how the `main_activity.xml` file will be rendered on round-faced Android Wear watches.

In order to provide the best user experience, you should make sure that the components are laid out and the users are able to access the UI elements without a problem. The only way we can do that is to test the app on various form factors and layout settings:

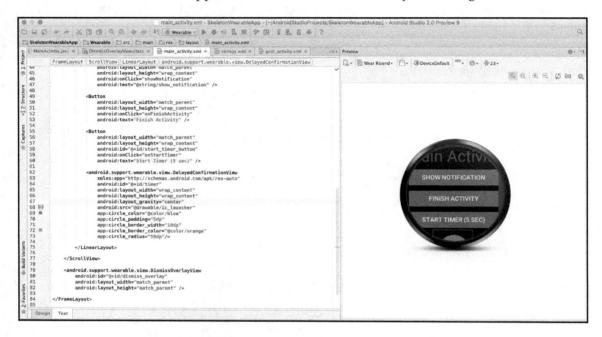

As we progress further through the book, we'll use techniques that will help serve both square-shaped and circle-shaped Android Wear devices by leveraging some Android support libraries.

By now, you'll have a basic understanding of how the skeleton wearable app was developed using some basic Android Wear API objects and components. Spend some time reading through `GridExampleActivity` and other parts of this project to get an idea of how all these pieces of the project are connected together.

If you don't follow much of the code in this project, do not fear. We'll be digging into all these aspects of Android Wear application development in later chapters of this book.

Let's build an Android Wear app

So far, we've been looking at the Skeleton wearable sample app that we cloned from Google's GitHub repository. We familiarized ourselves with how the skeleton app was structured and got some ideas of how the code and components are structured.

Now, it's time for us to build our own Android Wear app. We'll be using Android Studio to create this app from scratch.

From the Android Studio welcome screen, click on **Start a new Android Studio project** option as shown in the following screenshot:

Configure the project with an application name, domain, and package name that suits your system settings:

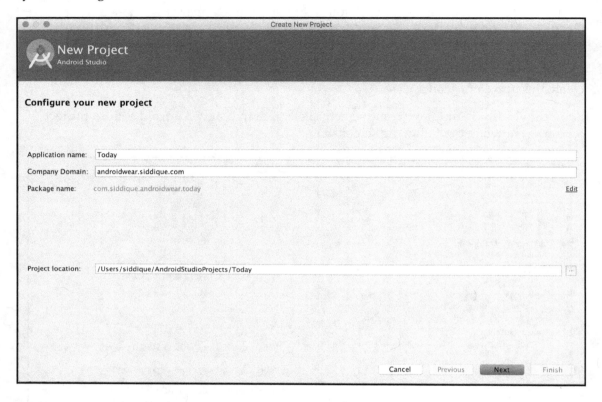

In the **Target Android Devices** screen, uncheck the **Phone and Tablet** option and make sure you select the **Wear** option. Android Studio will automatically select the safest minimum SDK needed to create the app based on the SDKs and system images you have installed on the system.

We're going to the default settings that were selected by Android Studio for this app:

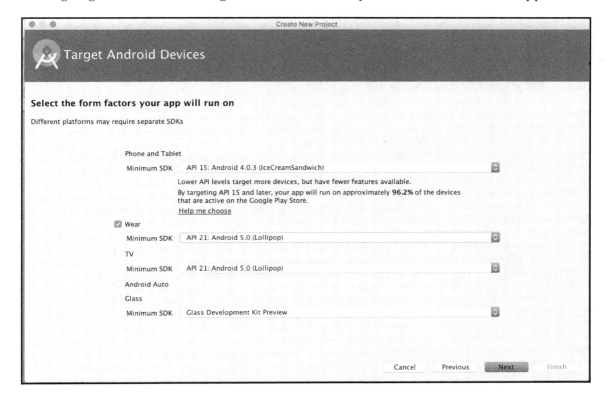

After you click the **Next** button, select **Blank Wear Activity**. By default, Android Studio will select **Always On Wear Activity**:

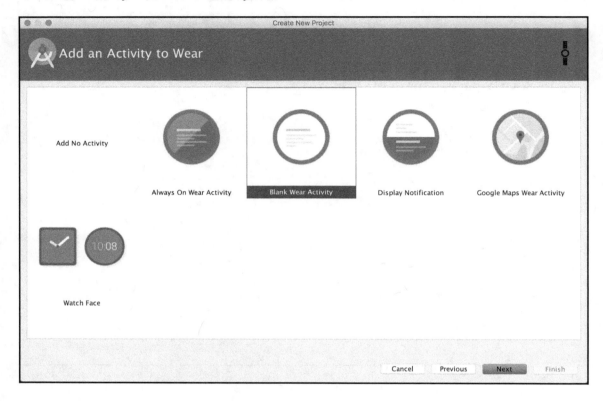

On the next screen, keep the activity name and other configurations unchanged:

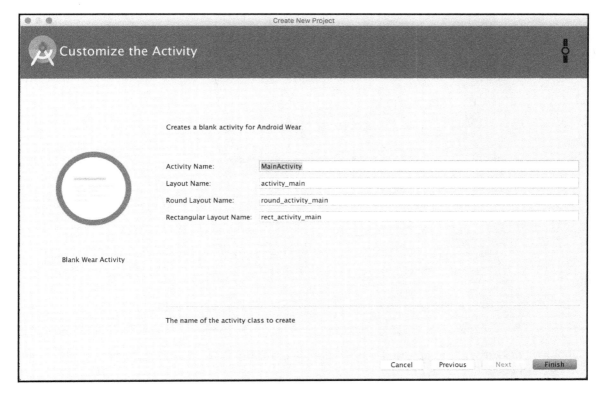

After you click on the **Finish** button, Android Studio will take some time to compile and build the project.

Once it's done, you'll see the project with `MainActivity` and three layout files, `activity_main.xml`, `rect_activity_main.xml`, and `round_activity_main.xml`.

Android Studio will also create a default run configuration for running the app:

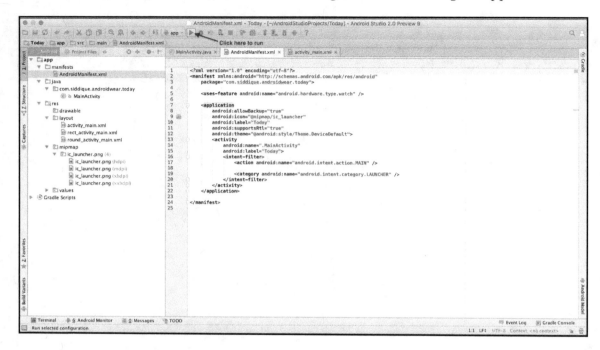

Clicking on **Run** will list all the Android device emulators. You can select one from the list we created earlier.

After you select the emulator, the device will boot up and the Android Studio will deploy the app to the emulator. Be patient at this stage, because it might take a while for the device to start and run the app we just built. Try not to interfere with the running emulator as it might cause issues running the app.

Although it might sound easy to develop an Android application using emulators, the frustrating part is the emulator's boot-up and application load times. If you have the option to develop using a physical device, go for that rather than wasting lots of time waiting and watching.

At some point during the course of this book, we'll be developing using a physical Android phone and a wearable device. We'll cover the settings and configurations needed to develop using those devices when we get there.

Here is a screenshot of how the screen looks after successfully running this app:

Let's add some customization to this project now. Update the onCreate method of the MainActivity file with the following code:

```
protected void onCreate(Bundle savedInstanceState){
  super.onCreate(savedInstanceState);
  setContentView(R.layout.activity_main);
  final WatchViewStub stub = (WatchViewStub)
findViewById(R.id.watch_view_stub);
  stub.setOnLayoutInflatedListener(new
WatchViewStub.OnLayoutInflatedListener()
  {
    @Override
    public void onLayoutInflated(WatchViewStub stub)
    {
      mTextView = (TextView) stub.findViewById(R.id.text);
      Date today = new Date();
      SimpleDateFormat dateFormat = new SimpleDateFormat("EEEE, MMMM d -
yyyy");mTextView.setText("Today is " + dateFormat.format(today));
    }
  });
}
```

What we are doing here is basically setting a dynamic text to mTextView component with the content saying today's date.

Update the `rect_activity_main.xml` file with the following content. We have just updated the background color of the layout and updated the text view's color and padding options:

```xml
<?xml version="1.0" encoding="utf-8"?>

<LinearLayout
  xmlns:android="http://schemas.android.com/apk/res/android"
  xmlns:tools="http://schemas.android.com/tools"
  android:layout_width="match_parent"
  android:layout_height="match_parent"
  android:orientation="vertical"
  tools:context="com.siddique.androidwear.today.MainActivity"
  tools:deviceIds="wear_square"
  android:background="@color/orange"
>

<TextView
  android:id="@+id/text"
  android:layout_width="wrap_content"
  android:layout_height="wrap_content"
  android:text="@string/hello_square"
  android:textSize="25sp"
  android:textAlignment="center"
  android:textColor="@color/black"
  android:paddingTop="25dp"
/>

</LinearLayout>
```

When you re-run the app, your output should look like the following screenshot:

 If you got stuck with any of the preceding steps, don't worry. The code we discussed is available on the GitHub repository (`https://github.com/siddii/mastering-android-wear/tree/master/Chapter_3`). Use that for reference or to compare against your project.

Summary

We discussed various components and aspects of our Android Wear project by going over the sample code from the skeleton wearable app. We looked at Android Studio's layout editor and saw how it was used to preview live updates to layout files.

We developed `Today`, an Android Wear app, from scratch using Android Studio. We'll be extending that app as we progress further through this book.

4
Developing Watch UI

"To create something exceptional, your mindset must be relentlessly focused on the smallest detail."

— *Giorgio Armani*

In this chapter, we will be extending the `Today` app, we started in the previous chapter using the UI components available in the Android Wear SDK. We will also be looking into building custom UI components using custom layouts that would fit into the watch's form factor.

We will be developing the `Today` app iteratively and incrementally as we go through the chapters in this book. We will be introducing various concepts and features of Android Wear SDKs and APIs when it's relevant, and utilizing them to make this app as feature-rich as possible.

Please note that by no means will the `Today` app be finished when we complete this chapter. It will be improved as we introduce more API concepts in further chapters.

 The code accompanying this chapter is available for reference on GitHub (`https://github.com/siddii/mastering-android-wear/tree/master/Chapter_4`).
For the sake of brevity, only code snippets are included as needed. The reader is encouraged to download the referenced code from GitHub and follow along as they progress through the chapter.

Wearable UI

By now, you probably realize that an Android Wear watch is not just a smaller form factor than its predecessors, such as the phone and tablet. There are various nuances and characteristics that make the Android Wear watch different to the other big screen devices.

First and foremost, there is no such thing as keyboard input, at least, not currently. That brings a major challenge in how you design apps for Android Wear platform. There is not much of interactivity available from the user due to the lack of keyboard (physical or virtual) data inputs.

On top of that, we also don't have the *ubiquitous* back button that is available on all other Android devices. The button for going back on the Android platform makes navigating inside an app and switching between apps a lot easier. Without that, it would be a lot harder to navigate within and between apps. The swipe gestures on the Android Wear watch are used like back buttons.

Before we start writing UI components and navigation code for the Android Wear app, if you are not very familiar with the Android Wear watch platform component and navigation flow, this would be a good time to spend some time on a physical device or emulator to see how they work. Poke around various stock apps and see how the swipe gestures and navigation work.

The important point to remember here is that, although the Android Wear device works differently to phones and tablets, it is running the same Android platform (operating system) available on every device. However, not all the UI components and widgets will be available or relevant to the Android Wear platform. It will be a subset of components, and in some cases, it will be a slimmed-down version of what is available on phones and tablets.

The Android manifest file

The `Today` app currently has two activities. The main activity is called `TodayActivity`, and the another one is `DayOfYearActivity`, which is used to display data specific to days of the year.

Note the use of the `uses-feature` tag, which makes it an Android Wear watch app:

```xml
<?xml version="1.0" encoding="utf-8"?>

<manifest
xmlns:android="http://schemas.android.com/apk/res/android"package="com.sidd
ique.androidwear.today">
```

```
<uses-feature android:name="android.hardware.type.watch" />

<application
  android:allowBackup="true"
  android:icon="@mipmap/ic_launcher"
  android:label="@string/app_name"
  android:supportsRtl="true"
  android:theme="@android:style/Theme.DeviceDefault">

<activity
  android:name=".TodayActivity"
  android:label="@string/app_name">
  <intent-filter>
    <action android:name="android.intent.action.MAIN" />
    <category android:name="android.intent.category.LAUNCHER" />
  </intent-filter>
</activity>

<activity
  android:name=".DayOfYearActivity"
  android:label="@string/day_of_year_card_title">
</activity>
</application>
</manifest>
```

The TodayActivity activity

Let's see what we have in the main activity–TodayActivity. In the onCreate method, we set the activity_main.xml layout as the content view. And we have WearableListView with action_list tied to the ListViewAdapter class.

Note that the TodayActivity activity also implements the click listener for the WearableListView class, which is why you see the onClick handler method implemented right next to the onCreate method.

At this point, the onClick listener method is handling only the first item in the list view. It launches DayOfYearActivity when it's clicked, and when the default Intent bundle is passed:

```
public class TodayActivity extends Activity implements
WearableListView.ClickListener
{
  private static final String TAG = TodayActivity.class.getName();

  @Override
```

```
   protected void onCreate(Bundle savedInstanceState)
   {
      super.onCreate(savedInstanceState);
      setContentView(R.layout.activity_main);
      WearableListView listView = (WearableListView)
findViewById(R.id.action_list);
      listView.setAdapter(new ListViewAdapter(this));
      listView.setClickListener(this);
   }

   @Override
   public void onClick(WearableListView.ViewHolder viewHolder)
   {
      Log.i(TAG, "Clicked list item" + viewHolder.getAdapterPosition());
      if (viewHolder.getAdapterPosition() == 0)
      {
        Intent intent = new Intent(this, DayOfYearActivity.class);
        startActivity(intent);
      }
   }

   @Override
   public void onTopEmptyRegionClick()
   {
      .. .
   }
   private static final class ListViewAdapter extends
WearableListView.Adapter
   {
      private final Context mContext;
      private final LayoutInflater mInflater;
      private String[] actions = null;
      private ListViewAdapter(Context context)
      {
        mContext = context;
        mInflater = LayoutInflater.from(context);
        actions = mContext.getResources().getStringArray(R.array.actions);
      }
      @Overridepublic
      WearableListView.ViewHolder onCreateViewHolder(ViewGroup parent, int
viewType)
      {
        return new
        WearableListView.ViewHolder(mInflater.inflate(R.layout.list_item,
null));
      }
      @Overridepublic
      void onBindViewHolder(WearableListView.ViewHolder holder, int position)
```

```
    {
      TextView view = (TextView) holder.itemView.findViewById(R.id.name);
      view.setText(actions[position]);
      holder.itemView.setTag(position);
    }

    @Overridepublic
    int getItemCount()
    {
      return actions.length;
    }
  }
}
```

Actions inside the arrays.xml file

The string values for the list view actions are declared inside the `arrays.xml` file. We can add more actions to this file as we improve or add features to this app:

```xml
<?xml version="1.0" encoding="utf-8"?>
<resources>
  <string-array name="actions">
    <item>Day of Year</item>
    <item>On this day...</item>
  </string-array>
</resources>
```

Main activity layout file

The layout file for the main activity, `activity_main.xml` is pretty simple. All it contains is the `WearableListView` component defined in the layout. As we mentioned earlier, the `WearableListView` component is an optimized version of the `ListView` method that is suitable for small screen devices. It handles all the scrolling and transitions needed while scrolling:

```xml
<?xml version="1.0"
encoding="utf-8"?><android.support.wearable.view.WearableListView
  xmlns:android="http://schemas.android.com/apk/res/android"
  android:id="@+id/action_list"
  android:layout_width="match_parent"
  android:layout_height="match_parent"
  android:scrollbars="none"
  android:dividerHeight="0dp"/>
```

When you launch the app using an Android Wear emulator, you should see the app listed with a custom launch icon, as shown in the following screenshot. Please note the icons for various device resolutions are placed in the `app/src/main/res/mipmap-*` folders:

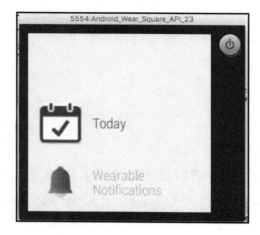

The WearableListItemLayout component

The `WearableListView` component is used to display a list of available actions in the app, whereas the `WearableListItemLayout` component is used to style or layout components in an individual list item.

In this specific case, we have `ImageView` and `TextView` tags. Note the usage of `android:src="@drawable/wl_circle"` line. It is essentially a drawable file available in the `res/drawable/wl_circle.xml` directory.

The `TextView` tag is used to display individual action strings that come from the `arrays.xml` file:

```
<com.siddique.androidwear.today.WearableListItemLayout

xmlns:android="http://schemas.android.com/apk/res/android"
android:gravity="center_vertical"
android:layout_width="match_parent"
android:layout_height="80dp">

<ImageView
  android:id="@+id/circle"
  android:layout_height="25dp"
  android:layout_margin="16dp"
```

```
    android:layout_width="25dp"
    android:src="@drawable/wl_circle"/>

  <TextView
    android:id="@+id/name"
    android:gravity="center_vertical|left"
    android:layout_width="wrap_content"
    android:layout_marginRight="16dp"
    android:layout_height="match_parent"
    android:fontFamily="sans-serif-condensed-light"
    android:lineSpacingExtra="-4sp"
    android:textColor="@color/text_color"
    android:textSize="16sp"/>

  </com.siddique.androidwear.today.WearableListItemLayout>
```

Here is the implementation of the `WearableListItemLayout` class. It is basically an extension of the `LinearLayout` class with some handler methods for the `OnCenterProximityListener` component of the `WearableListView` component. Take a moment to understand how the `colors` and `alpha` characteristics of the components are updated when the list items are scrolled and brought into the center position:

```
package com.siddique.androidwear.today;

import android.content.Context;
import android.graphics.drawable.GradientDrawable;
import android.support.wearable.view.WearableListView;
import android.util.AttributeSet;
import android.widget.ImageView;
import android.widget.LinearLayout;
import android.widget.TextView;

public class WearableListItemLayout extends LinearLayoutimplements
WearableListView.OnCenterProximityListener
{
  private final float mFadedTextAlpha;private final int mFadedCircleColor;
  private final int mChosenCircleColor;
  private ImageView mCircle;
  private TextView mName;
  public WearableListItemLayout(Context context)
  {
    this(context, null);
  }

  public WearableListItemLayout(Context context, AttributeSet attrs)
  {
```

```
      this(context, attrs, 0);
   }

   public WearableListItemLayout(Context context, AttributeSet attrs, int
defStyle)
   {
      super(context, attrs, defStyle);
      mFadedTextAlpha =
getResources().getInteger(R.integer.action_text_faded_alpha) / 10f;
      mFadedCircleColor = getResources().getColor(R.color.wl_gray);
      mChosenCircleColor = getResources().getColor(R.color.wl_orange);
   }

   @Override
   protected void onFinishInflate()
   {
      super.onFinishInflate();
      mCircle = (ImageView) findViewById(R.id.circle);
      mName = (TextView) findViewById(R.id.name);
   }

   @Override
   public void onCenterPosition(boolean animate)
   {
   mName.setAlpha(1f);
   ((GradientDrawable)
mCircle.getDrawable()).setColor(mChosenCircleColor);
   }

   @Override
   public void onNonCenterPosition(boolean animate)
   {
   ((GradientDrawable)
mCircle.getDrawable()).setColor(mFadedCircleColor);mName.setAlpha(mFadedTex
tAlpha);
   }
}
```

Here is a screenshot of the action list we can see:

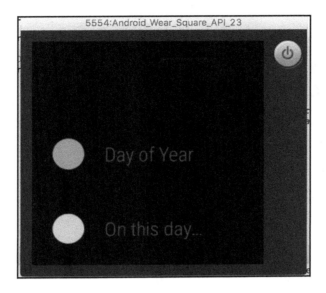

The DayOfYearActivity class

The DayOfYearActivity activity is a very simple class that uses Java's default java.util.Calendar instance to calculate how many days have passed and how many days are remaining until the end of the year:

```
import android.app.Activity;
import android.os.Bundle;
import android.widget.TextView;
import java.util.Calendar;

public class DayOfYearActivity extends Activity
{
  @Override
  protected void onCreate(Bundle savedInstanceState)
  {
  super.onCreate(savedInstanceState);
  setContentView(R.layout.activity_day_of_year);
  Calendar calendar = Calendar.getInstance();
  String dayOfYearDesc = getString(R.string.day_of_year_card_desc,
    calendar.get(Calendar.DAY_OF_YEAR),
    calendar.getActualMaximum(Calendar.DAY_OF_YEAR) -
    calendar.get(Calendar.DAY_OF_YEAR));
```

```
    TextView desc = (TextView) findViewById(R.id.day_of_year_desc);
    desc.setText(dayOfYearDesc);
    }
}
```

The activity_day_of_year.xml file

An interesting thing about the `BoxInsetLayout` component is that it's a screen-aware component that boxes its children in the center square. It's a safe component that tries to fit nicely on square or circular screens:

```xml
<android.support.wearable.view.BoxInsetLayout
    xmlns:android="http://schemas.android.com/apk/res/android"
    xmlns:app="http://schemas.android.com/apk/res-auto"
    android:layout_height="match_parent"
    android:layout_width="match_parent"
    android:background="@drawable/sunrise">

    <android.support.wearable.view.CardScrollView
        android:id="@+id/card_scroll_view"
        andoid:layout_height="match_parent"
        android:layout_width="match_parent"
        app:layout_box="bottom">

        <android.support.wearable.view.CardFrame
            android:layout_height="wrap_content"
            android:layout_width="fill_parent">

        <LinearLayout
            android:layout_height="wrap_content"
            android:layout_width="match_parent"
            android:orientation="vertical"
            android:paddingLeft="5dp">

        <TextView
            android:fontFamily="sans-serif-light"
            android:layout_height="wrap_content"
            android:layout_width="match_parent"
            android:text="@string/day_of_year_card_title"
            android:textColor="@color/black"
            android:textSize="18sp"/>

        <TextView
            android:id="@+id/day_of_year_desc"
            android:fontFamily="sans-serif-light"
            android:layout_height="wrap_content"
```

```
        android:layout_width="match_parent"
        android:text="@string/day_of_year_card_desc"
        android:textColor="@color/black"
        android:textSize="12sp"/>
    </LinearLayout>

    </android.support.wearable.view.CardFrame>
  </android.support.wearable.view.CardScrollView>
</android.support.wearable.view.BoxInsetLayout>
```

You can see the following action in the emulator:

As we build layout components it's a good idea to preview them in both circular and square profiles to see how good they look.

Take a look at the following screenshot to see how the day of year activity layout is displayed on a circular screen. Since we used the `BoxInsetLayout` layout component, it is rendered pretty decently on both square and circular screens:

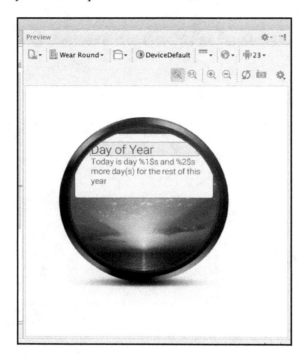

Here is the `DayOfYearActivity` activity in action. You can swipe right to go back to the previous activity, which is the main activity in this case:

Summary

We discussed how we could utilize list views and layouts that are specific to wearable devices. We developed a list of actions in our Today app and implemented actions for list items. We created an action handler that launches an activity from the main activity to display components in the BoxInsetLayout layout.

This is just a tiny use case that shows how we can utilize Android Wear UI components and customize them for our needs. We couldn't discuss all the files that were used in the sample app. Spend some time studying the sample code from this chapter. This will help you connect the dots and understand how the individual pieces come together.

We are now ready to step into more advanced topics in Wear development. This would be a good time to review the basics of how UI and layout components work together in general on the Android platform.

5
Synchronizing Data

"How we need another soul to cling to."
-Sylvia Plath

In the previous chapter, we walked you through creating a standalone wearable app. In this chapter, we introduce the idea of a companion handheld app, and why it is needed. We then walk you through the steps required to pair a handheld device with an Android Wear emulator to expand your environment for wearable app development.

We will then augment the Today app we started in the previous chapter with the ability to display *this day in history* by having it pull content from a public feed page via the companion app.

 The code samples for this chapter are available on GitHub (`https://githu b.com/siddii/mastering-android-wear/tree/master/Chapter_5`). Please use the actual code for reference as you follow along.

What is a companion app anyway?

Wearable apps run directly on the wearable device and in this way let you access the device's hardware, activities, and services all on the device itself. The breadth of operations that may be performed on a wearable device is limited by design, owing to the smaller scale and the need to efficiently manage processing power and memory. In addition to that, wearables don't support the Google Play store. In addition to that, Android Wear 1.x does not allow direct install of apps from the Google Play Store.

A companion handheld app addresses these concerns to let us benefit from a rich user experience on our wearable device. The point to remember is that a wearable app is packaged within a companion handheld app. The companion app is what gets published to the Google Play store, as described in the following figure:

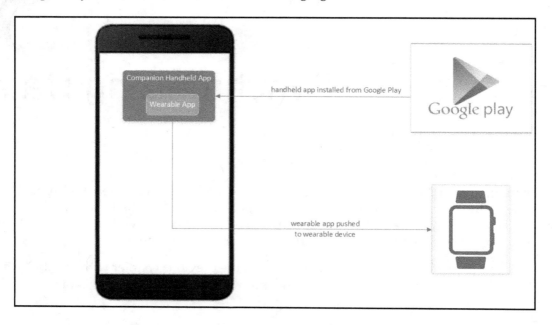

When users download the companion app to a handheld device, the wearable app within it is automatically pushed to all connected wearables, as described in the following figure:

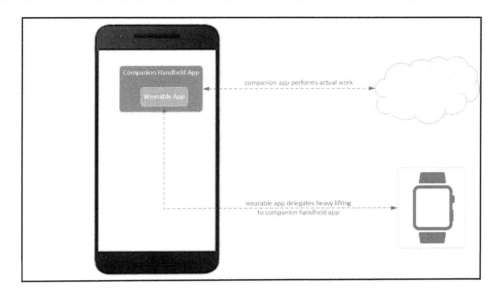

Furthermore, the companion app running on the handheld device is better suited to doing the heavy lifting involved when an app performs network actions, intensive computation, and other resource-intensive work. The companion app then sends results to the wearable, thus communicating the outcome of its operations.

Before we can create a project housing a companion app module along with its wearable app module, we need to set up our development environment to let us work with a wearable device on our handheld device.

It is expected that Android Wear 2.0 will change the way Wear apps are packaged and installed from Google Play store. The auto-installation for Wear apps in Wear 1.x is to be retired. Instead, Wear 2.0 apps are expected to have full network access and their installation is to be completely separate from that of handheld apps. Google is moving towards standalone wearable apps as the preferred packaging approach, but it is not clear yet whether standalone apps will be required (with no option for auto-installation) or if they will simply be supported as an additional feature.

Setting up an Android Wear virtual device

These steps are published on the Android Developers site (`https://developer.android.c om/training/wearables/apps/creating.html`), in the **Creating and Running a Wearable App** section. They are repeated here and expanded upon for convenience.

To set up an Android Wear virtual device, click **Tools | Android | AVD Manager** in Android Studio and perform the following steps:

1. Click on the **Create virtual device...** option.
2. Click **Wear** in the Category list:
    1. Select **Android Wear Square** or **Android Wear Round**.
    2. Click on the **Next** button.
    3. Select a release name (for example, KitKat Wear).
    4. Click **Next**.
    5. Change any preferences for your virtual device (optional).
    6. Click **Finish**.
3. Start the emulator:
    1. Select the virtual device you just created.
    2. Click the green play button.
    3. Wait until the emulator initializes and shows the Android Wear home screen.
4. Pair the Android handheld device with the Wearable emulator:
    1. On your handheld device, install the Android Wear app provided by Google from Google Play.
    2. Connect the handheld device to your machine via USB.
    3. Forward the AVD's communication port to the connected handheld device (you must do this every time the device is connected). If we don't see any errors after the following command run, then everything is fine:

4. Start the Android Wear app on your handheld device and connect to the emulator by selecting **Connect Emulator**, as shown in the following image:

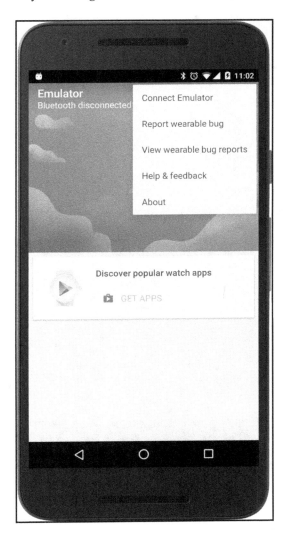

A successful connection is depicted in the following image:

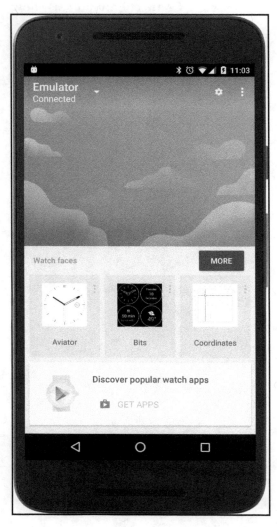

5. Launch the Settings menu and select **Try out watch notifications**:

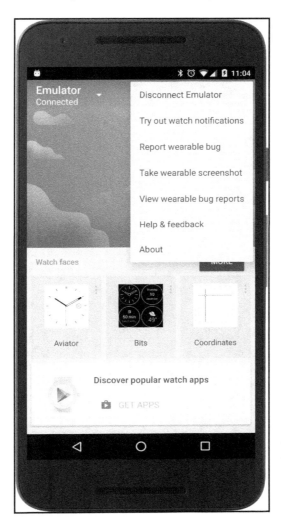

5. Select **Reminder (by time)** option from the list:

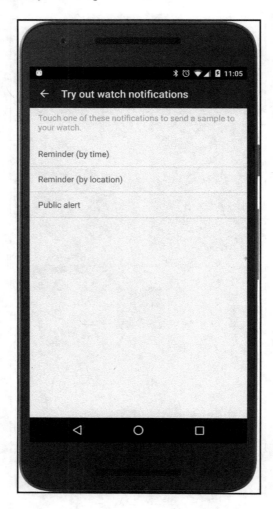

The following screen appears on the wearable emulator:

Revisiting the Today app

Now that we have the ability to work with a wearable device on our handheld, let's revisit the Today app we developed in the previous chapter.

That simplistic version of the app helped gets us started, no doubt. But it doesn't really cut it for us. In order to enjoy a fuller experience of a wearable device's capabilities, we need to expand our requirements. So, we've decided to devote the rest of this chapter to augmenting our Today app significantly.

We'll describe the features of the new app in a bit, but first, let's get started by creating a new project in Android Studio—one that includes a wearable app as well as a companion app; and setting it up with the sample code for this chapter.

We thought it might be refreshing to start over; that is why our new app is still named `Today`. Feel free to call it whatever you like:

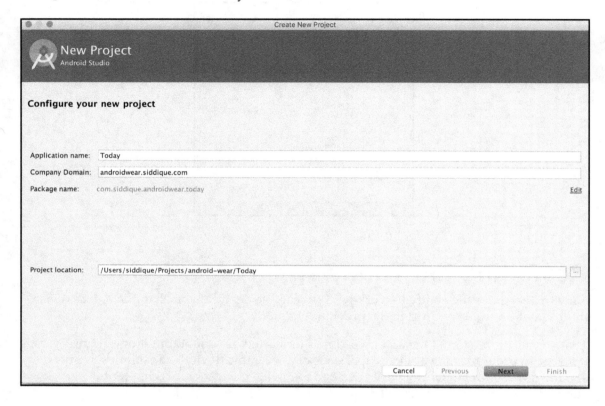

Be sure to select the form factors for the app as shown in the following screenshot–**Phone and Tablet**, and **Wear** :

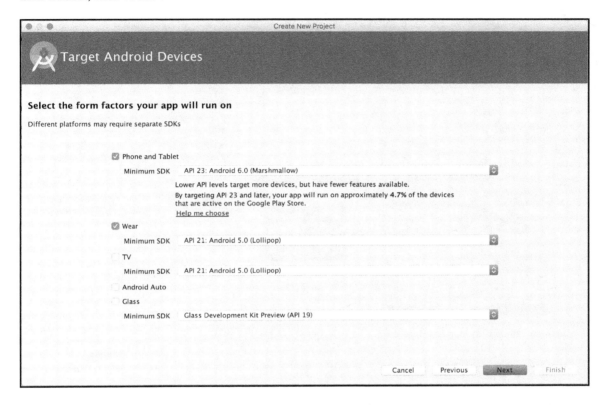

Add an empty activity to the **Mobile** module by clicking on **Empty Activity** :

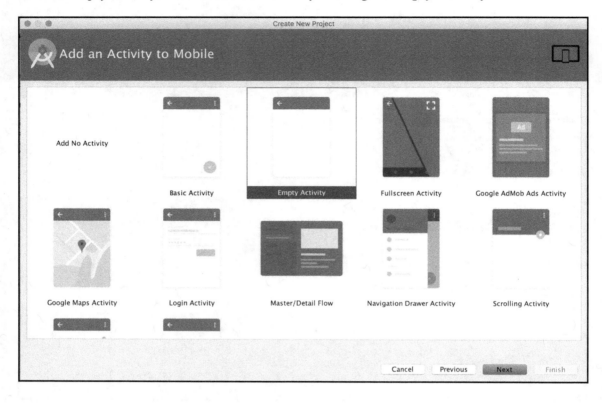

Give a suitable name to your activity in the following screen:

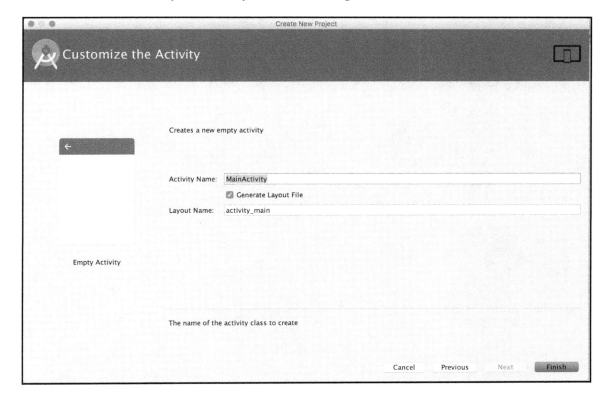

For now, choose the **Add No Activity** option in the **Wear** module, and click **Finish** :

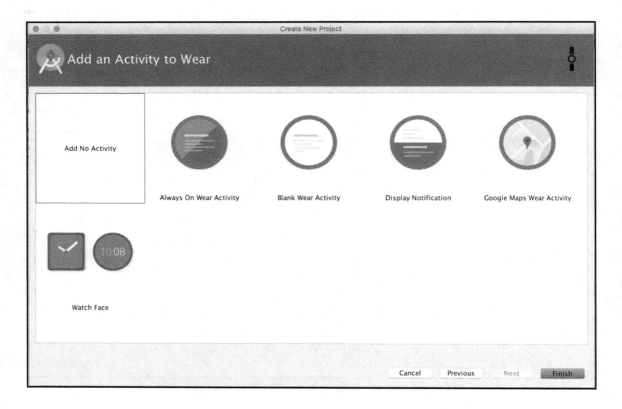

Android Studio creates the **Wear** and **Mobile** modules depicted in the following screenshot:

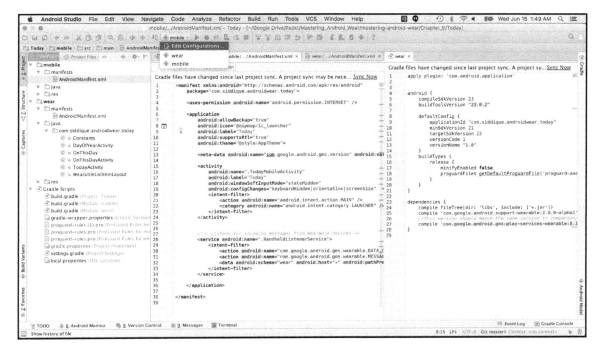

The preceding screenshot shows the state of our project. Note that Android Studio created two modules–mobile and wear. It also created Gradle scripts for them and added the necessary dependencies. Furthermore, the *run target* configuration for both modules was created as well.

We copied our code (that is, activities, resources, icons, and so on) from the `Today` project we created in `Chapter 4`, *Developing Watch UI*, into the wear module of this newly created project, and then augmented it to meet our expanded requirements. This is a good time to examine what those requirements are.

Scope of the new Today app

We all know how important dates are. Who doesn't get a kick out of learning that their significant other shares a birthday with a famous celebrity, or better yet, an infamous one? With that in mind, let's spruce up our `Today` app to do more than simply display the current date. Let's have it pull content from a public feed paged named *On This Day* (`https://en.wikipedia.org/wiki/Special:FeedItem/onthisday/20160615000000/en`), which shares one or more historically important events/occurrences whose anniversary happens to coincide with today.

This seems like a larger enough bite into the Wearable API stack that will let us study the interplay between a wearable device and its companion app without too much additional complexity.

Before we dive into the application code, it behooves us to cover a few concepts, tools, and API objects that are essential to our application. The intent here is to get you enough information to understand the core portions of the sample code. You can always come back and refer to this chapter and the documentation referenced in it.

The Wearable data layer API

Google Play services include a Wearable data layer API (`https://developer.android.com/training/wearables/data-layer/index.html`), through which your handheld and wearable apps may communicate with each other.

We encourage you to study the data layer API documentation located at the preceding page on Android developers site, but certain key data objects in the API deserve special attention.

MessageApi

This interface exposes methods for the wearables and handheld device to send messages to each other. Messages sent to connected network nodes (that is, paired devices) are queued for delivery. It is important to keep in mind that a message created by an application is private to that application and accessible only by that application running on other nodes.

WearableListenerService

This class should be extended by applications that expect to be notified of events while running in the background. Events include when a message is received, when data changes, and when nodes connect to or disconnect from the Android Wear network, which is the constantly shifting network of wearable devices and the handheld devices that they can connect to and/or interact with.

DataListener

While the `WearableListenerService` class notifies applications while they run in the background, the `DataListener` interface notifies applications implementing it of data layer events while they run in the foreground.

Cloud Node

Along with all of the user's connected devices (nodes), Google's servers implicitly host a cloud node in the network of devices. The purpose of the cloud nodes is to synchronize data between directly connected devices. Changes to an application's state on a handheld device are pushed to all of the user's wearable devices and vice versa as depicted in the following figure:

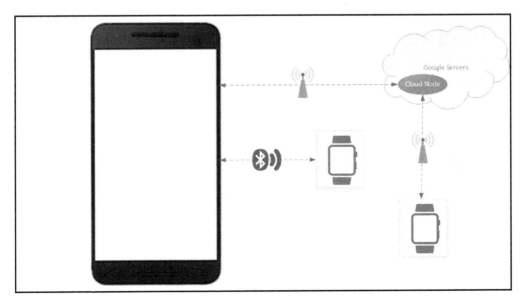

The GoogleApiClient class

We need to create an instance of the `GoogleApiClient` class, any time you want to make a connection to one of the Google APIs provided in the Google Play services library. The Google API client provides a common entry point to all Google Play services and manages the network connection between the user's device and each Google service.

We use this class to let our mobile device connect to the Wearable API in the Google Play services library in order to get access to connected wearables.

The Volley library

We will be using Volley to fetch HTML content from Wikipedia. You can read all about this HTTP library on the developer's web page (`https://developer.android.com/training/volley/index.html`).

The JSoup library

The JSoup library (`https://jsoup.org`) will be our preferred library to parse the HTML content feed that we pull from Wikipedia. Now, let's take a look at the code.

The Build Script

Study the dependencies specified in the `build.gradle` file of the mobile and companion apps respectively. Note how the mobile app's `build.gradle` file has the additional dependencies for `Volley` and `JSoup` libraries. Remember that the companion app has to do the heavy lifting:

```
dependencies {
    compile fileTree(dir: 'libs', include: ['*.jar'])
    wearApp project(':wear')
    testCompile 'junit:junit:4.12'
    compile 'com.android.support:appcompat-v7:23.4.0'
    compile 'com.google.android.support:wearable:2.0.0-alpha1'
    // This version should match the same version in wearable app
    compile 'com.google.android.gms:play-services-wearable:8.1.0'
    // Use volley to make HTTP requests
    compile 'com.android.volley:volley:1.0.0'
    // Use JSoup for parsing HTML data
    compile "org.jsoup:jsoup:1.8.1"
}
```

Companion app's Android manifest file

Please have a look at the `AndroidManifest.xml` file of the companion app with a basic `TodayMobileActivity` and `HandheldListenerService` activities:

```xml
<manifest xmlns:android="http://schemas.android.com/apk/res/android"
package="com.siddique.androidwear.today">
  <uses-permission android:name="android.permission.INTERNET" />
  <application
    android:allowBackup="true"
    android:icon="@mipmap/ic_launcher"
    android:label="@string/app_name"
    android:supportsRtl="true"
    android:theme="@style/AppTheme">

  <meta-data
    android:name="com.google.android.gms.version"
    android:value="@integer/google_play_services_version" />

  <activity
    android:name=".TodayMobileActivity"
    android:label="@string/app_name"
    android:windowSoftInputMode="stateHidden"
    android:configChanges="keyboardHidden|orientation|screenSize"  >

    <intent-filter>
      <action android:name="android.intent.action.MAIN" />
      <category android:name="android.intent.category.LAUNCHER" />
    </intent-filter>
  </activity>

<!-- Listens for incoming messages from Wearable devices-->

  <service android:name=".HandheldListenerService">
    <intent-filter>
      <action android:name="com.google.android.gms.wearable.DATA_CHANGED"
/>
      <action
android:name="com.google.android.gms.wearable.MESSAGE_RECEIVED" />
      <data
        android:scheme="wear"
        android:host="*"
        android:pathPrefix="/today" />
    </intent-filter>
  </service>
  </application>
</manifest>
```

The TodayMobileActivity class

The `TodayMobileActivity` class is a convenience activity at this time, intended only to connect to any existing wearable devices paired with the mobile device. We will be running the mobile/companion app target on a mobile device:

```java
public class TodayMobileActivity extends Activity implements
GoogleApiClient.ConnectionCallbacks,
GoogleApiClient.OnConnectionFailedListener
{
  private GoogleApiClient mGoogleApiClient;
  public static final String TAG = TodayMobileActivity.class.getName();
  private int CONNECTION_TIME_OUT_MS = 15000;
  private TextView devicesConnectedTextView = null;
  @Override
  protected void onCreate(Bundle savedInstanceState)
  {
    super.onCreate(savedInstanceState);
    setContentView(R.layout.main);
    Log.i(TAG, "Creating Google Api Client");
    mGoogleApiClient = new GoogleApiClient.Builder(this)
      .addApi(Wearable.API)
      .addConnectionCallbacks(this)
      .addOnConnectionFailedListener(this)
      .build();
    devicesConnectedTextView = (TextView)
findViewById(R.id.devicesConnected);
  }

  @Override
  protected void onStart()
  {
    super.onStart();
    if (!mGoogleApiClient.isConnected())
    {
      mGoogleApiClient.connect();
    }
  }
  @Override
  public void onConnected(Bundle connectionHint)
  {
    Log.i(TAG, "Google Api Client Connected");
    new Thread(new Runnable()
    {
      @Override
      public void run()
      {
```

```
        mGoogleApiClient.blockingConnect(CONNECTION_TIME_OUT_MS,
TimeUnit.MILLISECONDS);
        NodeApi.GetConnectedNodesResult result =
Wearable.NodeApi.getConnectedNodes(mGoogleApiClient).await();
        final List<Node> nodes = result.getNodes();
        runOnUiThread(new Runnable()
        {
        public void run()
        {
          Log.i(TAG, "Connected devices = " + nodes.size());
          devicesConnectedTextView.setText(String.valueOf(nodes.size()));
        }
      });
    }
  }).
  start();
  }
  ...
}
```

Once we successfully connect with the wearable device, we should be able to see a confirmation that at least one device is connected, as shown in the following figure:

Users can launch the `TodayMobileActivity` class to see if the devices are connected or not. If the value shown against Devices connected is not greater than zero, then the mobile device is not paired successfully, meaning it is not connected to the wearable device or emulator. We will be expanding this activity more in future chapters.

Wearable app's Android manifest file

Here is the `AndroidManifest.xml` file for the wearable app with the three activities for the menu items, such as the `TodayActivity`, `DayOfYearActivity`, and `OnThisDayActivity` activities:

```
<manifest
xmlns:android="http://schemas.android.com/apk/res/android"package="com.sidd
ique.androidwear.today">
  <uses-feature android:name="android.hardware.type.watch" />
  <application
    android:allowBackup="true"
    android:icon="@mipmap/ic_launcher"
    android:label="@string/app_name"
    android:supportsRtl="true"
    android:theme="@android:style/Theme.DeviceDefault">

<!-- We need this entry to use Google Play Services -->

  <meta-data
    android:name="com.google.android.gms.version"
    android:value="@integer/google_play_services_version" />

  <activity
    android:name=".TodayActivity"
    android:label="@string/app_name">
    <intent-filter>
      <action android:name="android.intent.action.MAIN" />
      <category android:name="android.intent.category.LAUNCHER" />
    </intent-filter>
  </activity>

  <activity
    android:name=".DayOfYearActivity"
    android:label="@string/day_of_year_card_title" />

  <activity
    android:name=".OnThisDayActivity"
    android:label="@string/on_this_day_title" />
  </application>
```

```
</manifest>
```

The OnThisDayActivity class

The `OnThisDayActivity` class sends a message to the mobile device (that is, the companion app) using the `GoogleApiClient` API, saying that it needs to fetch content from Wikipedia.

Take note of the `onDataChanged` handler method defined in this activity. The `onDataChanged` method is the callback listener that gets processed when the companion app sends data packets back to the wearable device:

```
public class OnThisDayActivity extends Activity
implementsDataApi.DataListener, GoogleApiClient.ConnectionCallbacks,
GoogleApiClient.OnConnectionFailedListener
{
  private GoogleApiClient mGoogleApiClient;private boolean mResolvingError;
  private static final String TAG = OnThisDayActivity.class.getName();
  private OnThisDay onThisDay = null;
  @Override
  protected void onCreate(Bundle savedInstanceState)
  {
    super.onCreate(savedInstanceState);
    setContentView(R.layout.activity_on_this_day);
    if (onThisDay == null)
    {
      Toast.makeText(this, "Fetching from Wikipedia...",
Toast.LENGTH_LONG).show();
      mGoogleApiClient = new GoogleApiClient.Builder(this)
        .addApi(Wearable.API)
        .addConnectionCallbacks(this)
        .addOnConnectionFailedListener(this)
        .build();
    }
    else
    {
      showOnThisDay(onThisDay);
    }
  }
  @Override
  protected void onStart()
  {
    super.onStart();
    if (!mResolvingError && onThisDay == null)
    {
      Log.i(TAG, "Connecting to Google Api Client");
```

```
        mGoogleApiClient.connect();
    }
    else
    {
        showOnThisDay(onThisDay);
    }
  }
  @Override
  public void onConnected(Bundle connectionHint)
  {
    Log.i(TAG, "Connected to Data Api");
    Wearable.DataApi.addListener(mGoogleApiClient, this);
// send a message to the companion app that it needs to fetch data
    sendMessage(Constants.ON_THIS_DAY_REQUEST, "OnThisDay".getBytes());
  }
  private void sendMessage(final String path, final byte[] data)
  {
    Log.i(TAG, "Sending message to path " + path);
 Wearable.NodeApi.getConnectedNodes(mGoogleApiClient).setResultCallback
(new ResultCallback<NodeApi.GetConnectedNodesResult>()
    {
    @Override
    public void onResult(NodeApi.GetConnectedNodesResult nodes)
    {
        for (Node node : nodes.getNodes())
        {
          Wearable.MessageApi.sendMessage(mGoogleApiClient, node.getId(),
path, data);
        }
    }
  });
  }

@Override
public void onConnectionSuspended(int i)
{
  Log.i(TAG, "Connection Suspended");
}

@Override
protected void onStop()
{
  if (null != mGoogleApiClient && mGoogleApiClient.isConnected())
  {
    Wearable.DataApi.removeListener(mGoogleApiClient, this);
    mGoogleApiClient.disconnect();
  }
  super.onStop();
```

```
  }
  @Override
  public void onDataChanged(DataEventBuffer dataEvents)
  {
    Log.i(TAG, "###### onDataChanged");
    for (DataEvent event : dataEvents)
    {
    if (event.getType() == DataEvent.TYPE_CHANGED)
    {
      DataItem dataItem = event.getDataItem();
      DataMap dataMap = DataMapItem.fromDataItem(dataItem).getDataMap();
      String heading = dataMap.get(Constants.ON_THIS_DAY_DATA_ITEM_HEADER);
      ArrayList<String> listItems =
  dataMap.get(Constants.ON_THIS_DAY_DATA_ITEM_CONTENT);
      onThisDay = new OnThisDay(heading, listItems);
      showOnThisDay(onThisDay);
      }
    }
  }
  private void showOnThisDay(OnThisDay onThisDay)
  {
    TextView heading = (TextView) findViewById(R.id.on_this_day_heading);
    heading.setText(Html.fromHtml(onThisDay.getHeadingHtml()));
    TextView content = (TextView) findViewById(R.id.on_this_day_content);
    content.setText(Html.fromHtml(onThisDay.getListItemsHtml()));
  }

  @Override
  public void onConnectionFailed(@NonNull ConnectionResult connectionResult)
  {
    Log.i(TAG, "Connection Failed " + connectionResult);
    mResolvingError = true;
    }
  }
```

The HandheldListenerService class

The HandheldListenerService class listens for messages coming from the wearable device. When a message is received, the onMessageReceived handler checks to see if the message is a request for content and if it is, it invokes a helper to read the feed and parse the response accordingly:

```
public class HandheldListenerService extends WearableListenerService
implements GoogleApiClient.ConnectionCallbacks,
GoogleApiClient.OnConnectionFailedListener
{
```

```
...
@Override
public void onMessageReceived(MessageEvent messageEvent)
{
  super.onMessageReceived(messageEvent);
  Log.i(TAG, "Message received" + messageEvent);
  if (Constants.ON_THIS_DAY_REQUEST.equals(messageEvent.getPath()))
  {
    //read Today's content from Wikipedia
    getOnThisDayContentFromWikipedia();
  }
}
private void getOnThisDayContentFromWikipedia()
{
  // Instantiate the RequestQueue
  RequestQueue queue = Volley.newRequestQueue(this);
  String url =
"https://en.wikipedia.org/wiki/Special:FeedItem/onthisday/" +
DATE_FORMAT.format(new Date()) + "000000/en";
  // Request a string response from the provided URL.
  StringRequest stringRequest = new StringRequest(Request.Method.GET,
url,new Response.Listener<String>()
    {
      @Override
      public void onResponse(String response)
      {
        Log.i(TAG, "Wikipedia response  = " + response);
        Document doc = Jsoup.parse(response);
        Element heading = doc.select("h1").first();
        Log.i(TAG, "Heading node = " + heading);if (heading != null)
        {
          Log.i(TAG, "Wikipedia page heading = " + heading);
          PutDataMapRequest dataMapRequest =
PutDataMapRequest.create(Constants.ON_THIS_DAY_DATA_ITEM_HEADER);
          DataMap dataMap = dataMapRequest.getDataMap();
// We add a timestamp is to make this dataMap 'dirty'. This lets the
wearable get updates
          dataMap.putLong(Constants.ON_THIS_DAY_TIMESTAMP, new
Date().getTime());
          dataMap.putString(Constants.ON_THIS_DAY_DATA_ITEM_HEADER,
heading.text());
          Element listNode = doc.select("ul").first();if (listNode != null)
        {
        Elements itemNodes = listNode.select("li");int size =
itemNodes.size();
        ArrayList<String> items = new ArrayList<String>();for (int i = 0; i
< size; i++)
        {
```

```
            items.add(itemNodes.get(i).text());
        }
      dataMap.putStringArrayList(Constants.ON_THIS_DAY_DATA_ITEM_CONTENT,
items);
      }
    Log.i(TAG, "Sending dataMap request ...");
    PendingResult<DataApi.DataItemResult> pendingResult =
Wearable.DataApi.putDataItem(mGoogleApiClient,
dataMapRequest.asPutDataRequest());
    PendingResult.setResultCallback(new
ResultCallback<DataApi.DataItemResult>()
      {
        @Override
        public void onResult(final DataApi.DataItemResult result)
        {
          if (result.getStatus().isSuccess())
          {
           Log.d(TAG, "Data item set: " + result.getDataItem().getUri());
          }
        }
      });
    }
  }
  },
  new Response.ErrorListener()
  {
    @Override
    public void onErrorResponse(VolleyError error)
    {
      Log.e(TAG, "Error reading online content = " + error);
    }
  });
  // Add the request to the RequestQueue.
  queue.add(stringRequest);
  }
```

As you can see, the code snippets provided here are incomplete and are intended only as a quick reference. You are encouraged to download and play with the latest code from GitHub.

If you run the app on your wearable device, this is what you will see:

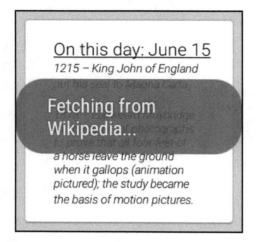

As you can see in the preceding screenshot, we show a *Toast* message while requesting to fetch *On This Day* content from Wikipedia using the handheld device's companion app:

Note that in our `activity_on_this_day` XML layout, we nest our `TextView` layout within a `ScrollView` layout, which effectively allows us to scroll through all of our feed items. This begs a discussion of the UX aspects of wearable app development. We can certainly utilize better UI components to do what we just did. More on this in future chapters.

Messages not coming through to your Wear app?

This can be frustrating, which is why we thought to mention it. If you see any synchronization issues whereby messages are not coming through to your wear application, check that the version of your Google Play services module matches between your companion app and wearable app `AndroidManifest.xml` files. Having different versions can lead to this sort of unexpected behavior and cost you hours in wasteful debugging. Consider the following screenshot of the Android Studio window:

Summary

We described the need for a companion handheld app and stepped through creating an Android Wear virtual device and pairing a handheld device with it. We then created a new Today app that pulls content from a public feed page via the companion app and pushes results to the wearable device.

In the next chapter, we will introduce context-aware notifications and voice interactions, which power a rich user experience with Android Wear.

6

Contextual Notifications

"Life is about timing."
– Carl Lewis

In this chapter, we will discuss notifications in Android Wear. After a quick comparison between notifications in wearable and handheld devices, we will continue extending the `Today` app from the previous chapter to demonstrate the Android Wear notifications API.

 The code accompanying this chapter is available for reference on GitHub (`https://github.com/siddii/mastering-android-wear/tree/master /Chapter_6`). For the sake of brevity, only code snippets are included as needed. The reader is encouraged to download the referenced code from GitHub and follow along as they progress through the chapter.

Getting notified

It should come as no surprise that wearable devices are naturally superior to handheld devices in their capacity to deliver notifications to the user. With a handheld device, you hear a beep, and you need to draw your device out from your purse or pocket or whatever choice holster you snagged at that recent eBay auction.

But with a smartwatch, things are quite different. When you hear that beep, you simply glance at your wrist. This ease is a hallmark feature of wearable device technology.

And it doesn't end there. With the help of voice interactions, the user can act on that notification by issuing a recognizable voice command. The voice interactions API, of course, predates the Wear API and has been in use on handheld devices for some time. But there is no denying the immense value it brings to wearable devices, fitting in perfectly with that ease of access. We'll deal with voice interactions in the next chapter.

So central is the notification model to wearable devices that most tutorials often introduce notifications as the core use case of Android Wear; the other features come later. We, obviously, chose a different treatment in this book. Here we are, spanning the halfway point in our book as we encounter the first serious discussion on notifications.

We did that, because notification, no matter how important or central they may be, are still an application feature, and thus secondary to the core functionality of an app. Delving into notifications without the benefit of being exposed to the nuts and bolts of an Android Wear app, in our opinion, would be putting the cart before the horse.

You've seen the barebones `Today` app, and you've augmented it to work with a companion handheld app. That's some good exposure to the Wear API. Now, you're ready to build upon that knowledge. Rest assured, if you've followed along so far, you will not find the notifications API intimidating by any means.

Enough talk; let's begin by introducing the core classes in the API before we get to see them in action in our sample application.

Core classes of the notifications API

Here are the core classes of the notifications API that we will be using in our application.

NotificationCompat.Builder

One thing you want when working with notifications on wearable devices is some sort of assurance that your notifications appear acceptable on the significantly reduced scale of a smart watch. That is where the notification builder class comes in. This class takes care of displaying notifications properly, whether they appear on a handheld or wearable device.

To use the notification builder, you will have to add the following line to your `build.gradle` file:

```
compile "com.android.support:support-v4:20.0.+"
```

Then you'll need to import the following core classes from the support library:

```
import android.support.v4.app.NotificationCompat;
import android.support.v4.app.NotificationManagerCompat;
import android.support.v4.app.NotificationCompat.WearableExtender;
```

Creating a notification then becomes a matter of instantiating the `NotificationCompat.Builder` class and issuing the notification, as we will see in our sample application.

Action buttons in your notification

The `addAction` method lets you add an action to the notification. Simply pass in a `PendingIntent` instance to the `addAction` method. While this action appears on a handheld as an additional button attached to the notification, on a wearable device it appears as a large button when the user swipes the notification to the left. Tapping the action invokes the associated intent on the handheld.

Wearable-only actions

If you want the actions available on the wearable to be different than those on the handheld, use the `addAction` method on the `NotificationCompat.WearableExtender` class. Doing so ensures that the wearable does not display actions added to the `NotificationCompat.Builder.addAction` class.

Delivery

Use the `NotificationManagerCompat` API instead of `NotificationManager` to deliver your notification, shown as follows. This ensures compatibility with older platforms:

```
// Get an instance of the NotificationManager service
NotificationManagerCompat notificationManager =
NotificationManagerCompat.from(mContext);

// Issue the notification with notification manager
notificationManager.notify(notificationId, notif);
```

Today app with to-do notifications

We are going to augment our `Today` app with a to-do activity that lets the user add to-do items and associate them with specific locations, such as home, or work. The locations then provide the context, which drives the notifications. This, in effect, makes our notifications *context-aware*.

For example, if the system detects that the user is in close proximity to the Home location, then to-do items associated with the `Home` category are presented to the user via the notifications API.

Geofencing

We'll be using the `Geofencing` API to figure out the location, that is, the context. In essence, this API lets us draw a circle of some agreed-upon radius around a coordinate. In effect, the latitude, longitude, and radius together define a *geofence*, a circular region around the coordinates of interest. Entrance and exit events signal when the device enters or exits the geofence location. An optional duration attribute delays the triggering of an event for that time interval once the device has entered and remained within the geofence.

You can study the `Geofencing` API in detail by visiting `https://developer.android.com/training/location/geofencing.html`.

Mocking a GPS

It is important to mention at the outset that it is not easy to simulate the location/GPS sensor behavior on a wearable device emulator, which all our sample code uses. A physical device equipped with GPS is needed for that. Furthermore, even if we did have access to a fully functional GPS, we could potentially run into frustrating scenarios testing our app–consider having to move physically to a different location in order to trigger the GPS sensors.

Hence, for the purposes of demonstrating context-aware notifications, we need a GPS mocking service that lets us use our wearable device emulator along with the physical handheld device, yet simulate different locations on demand.

This is where ByteRev's **FakeGPS** application comes into play (`https://play.google.com/store/apps/details?id=com.lexa.fakegps&hl=en`).

This free app lets us mock different locations and effectively gives us the equivalent experience of working with a fully functional GPS unit on a physical device. The downside is that the user may need to rerun the app in order to simulate the intended behavior. But that is an acceptable trade-off for flexibility.

The build.gradle file on wear and mobile apps

The `build.gradle` file of the mobile handheld app should contain the following line for location services:

```
compile 'com.google.android.gms:play-services-location:9.0.2'
```

Both wear and mobile apps should contain the following compile dependencies for notification support:

```
compile 'com.android.support:support-v13:23.4.0'
```

Handheld app's Android manifest file

Note the permission grant that allows the app to access a precise location, that is, a latitude and longitude coordinate:

```xml
<?xml version="1.0" encoding="utf-8"?>
<manifest  xmlns:android="http://schemas.android.com/apk/res/android"
  package="com.siddique.androidwear.today">

  <uses-sdk  android:minSdkVersion = "18" android:targetSdkVersion="22"/>

  <uses-permission  android:name = "android.permission.INTERNET"/>

  <uses-permission  android:name="android.permission.ACCESS_FINE_LOCATION"
/>

<application
  android:allowBackup="true"
  android:icon="@mipmap/ic_launcher"
  android:label="@string/app_name"
  android:supportsRtl="true"
  android:theme="@style/AppTheme">
  <meta-data
    android:name="com.google.android.gms.version"
    android:value="@integer/google_play_services_version"
  />

  <activity
    android:name=".TodayMobileActivity"
    android:configChanges="keyboardHidden|orientation|screenSize"
    android:label="@string/app_name"
    android:windowSoftInputMode="stateHidden">
  </activity>

<!-- Listens for incoming messages from Wearable devices -->
  <service android:name=".HandheldListenerService">
    <intent-filter>

      <action
android:name="com.google.android.gms.wearable.DATA_CHANGED"/>
      <action
android:name="com.google.android.gms.wearable.MESSAGE_RECEIVED"/>

      data
        android:host="*"
        android:pathPrefix="/today"
        android:scheme="wear" />
    </intent-filter>
```

```
    </service>

    <activity
        android:name=".TodoMobileActivity"
        android:label="@string/title_activity_todo_mobile"
        android:theme="@style/AppTheme.NoActionBar">
        <intent-filter>
            <action android:name="android.intent.action.MAIN" />

    <category android:name="android.intent.category.LAUNCHER" />
        </intent-filter>
    </activity>

    <service
        android:name=".GeofenceTransitionsIntentService"
        android:exported="false">
    </service>
    </application>
</manifest>
```

We added new activity called `TodoMobileActivity` to let us add to-do items. Since we will need to access the GPS sensor, the `ACCESS_FINE_LOCATION` permission becomes necessary to this new activity.

The `GeofenceTransitionsIntentService` service will react to the changes in location.

The TodoMobileActivity class

The `TodoMobileActivity` class is a simple activity that presents the user with a list view and capability to add to-do items. Each item added might be associated with a known set of locations (home or work), each of which is hardwired to a GPS coordinate:

```
public class TodoMobileActivity extends AppCompatActivity implements
GoogleApiClient.ConnectionCallbacks,
GoogleApiClient.OnConnectionFailedListener
{
    private ListView mTaskListView;
    private ArrayAdapter<String> mAdapter;

      public static final String TAG =  TodoMobileActivity.class.getName();
    private List<Geofence> geofenceList;
    private PendingIntent mGeofencePendingIntent;    private GoogleApiClient
mGoogleApiClient;

    @Override
    protected void onCreate(Bundle savedInstanceState)
```

```
    {
        super.onCreate(savedInstanceState);
        setContentView(R.layout.activity_todo_mobile);
        Toolbar toolbar = (Toolbar) findViewById(R.id.toolbar);
        setSupportActionBar(toolbar);

        mTaskListView = (ListView) findViewById(R.id.list_todo);
refreshItems();

        FloatingActionButton fab = (FloatingActionButton)
findViewById(R.id.addTodo);
        if (fab != null) {
        fab.setOnClickListener(new View.OnClickListener()
        {
          @Override        public void onClick(View view)
          {
            LayoutInflater inflater = (LayoutInflater)
getSystemService(Context.LAYOUT_INFLATER_SERVICE);
            final View addTodoItemView =
inflater.inflate(R.layout.add_todo_item, null);

            final Spinner spinner = (Spinner)
addTodoItemView.findViewById(R.id.todoItemType);
            ArrayAdapter<CharSequence> adapter =
ArrayAdapter.createFromResource(TodoMobileActivity.this,
R.array.todoItemTypes, android.R.layout.simple_spinner_item);
            adapter.setDropDownViewResource(
android.R.layout.simple_spinner_dropdown_item);
            spinner.setAdapter(adapter);

            AlertDialog dialog = new
AlertDialog.Builder(TodoMobileActivity.this)
            .setTitle("Add a new todo item")        .setView(addTodoItemView)
.setPositiveButton("Add", new  DialogInterface.OnClickListener()
            {
              @Override
              public void onClick(DialogInterface dialog, int which)
              {
                EditText taskEditText = (EditText)
addTodoItemView.findViewById(R.id.todoItem);
                Log.i(TAG, "Todo Item = " + taskEditText.getText());

                Spinner todoItemTypeSpinner = (Spinner)
addTodoItemView.findViewById(R.id.todoItemType);
                String todoItemType = (String)
todoItemTypeSpinner.getSelectedItem();
                Log.i(TAG, "Todo Item type = " + todoItemType);
```

```
              String task = String.valueOf(taskEditText.getText());
              Set<String> todoItems =
TodoItems.readItems(TodoMobileActivity.this, todoItemType);
todoItems.add(task);
              TodoItems.saveItems(TodoMobileActivity.this, todoItemType,
todoItems);
              refreshItems();
          }
      })
      .setNegativeButton("Cancel", null)
      .create();
       dialog.show();
    }
  });
  }

  if(null == mGoogleApiClient)
  {
    mGoogleApiClient = new GoogleApiClient.Builder(this)
    .addApi(LocationServices.API)
    .addConnectionCallbacks(this)
    .addOnConnectionFailedListener(this)
    .build();
     Log.i(TAG, "GoogleApiClient created");
  }

  if(!mGoogleApiClient.isConnected())
  {
    mGoogleApiClient.connect();
    Log.i(TAG, "Connecting to GoogleApiClient..");
  }
}

private void createGeofences()
{
  Log.i(TAG, "Creating geo fences");
  geofenceList = new ArrayList<Geofence>();
  geofenceList.add(new SimpleGeofence(
    Constants.HOME_GEOFENCE_ID,
    Constants.HOME_LATITUDE,
    Constants.HOME_LONGITUDE).toGeofence());

  geofenceList.add(new SimpleGeofence(
    Constants.WORK_GEOFENCE_ID,
    Constants.WORK_LATITUDE,
    Constants.WORK_LONGITUDE).toGeofence());
}
```

```java
private void refreshItems()
{
  ArrayList<String> taskList = new ArrayList<>();

  String[] todoItemTypes =
getResources().getStringArray(R.array.todoItemTypes);
  for (String todoItemType : todoItemTypes)
  {
    Set<String> todoItems = TodoItems.readItems(this,
todoItemType);
    for (String todoItem : todoItems)
    {
      taskList.add(todoItemType + " - " + todoItem);
    }
  }

  if (mAdapter == null) {
    mAdapter = new ArrayAdapter<>(this,
    R.layout.item_todo,
    R.id.task_title,
    taskList);
    mTaskListView.setAdapter(mAdapter);    }
  else
  {
    mAdapter.clear();
    mAdapter.addAll(taskList);
    mAdapter.notifyDataSetChanged();
  }
}

public void deleteTodoItem(View view)
{
  View parent = (View) view.getParent();
  TextView textView = (TextView)  parent.findViewById(R.id.task_title);

  String removingItem = (String) textView.getText();
  Log.i(TAG, "Removing Item = " + removingItem);

  String[] todoItemTypes =
getResources().getStringArray(R.array.todoItemTypes);
  TodoItems.removeItem(this, todoItemTypes, removingItem);
  refreshItems();
}

@Override public void onConnected(@Nullable Bundle bundle)
{
  if(mGoogleApiClient != null)
  {
```

```
    mGeofencePendingIntent = getGeofenceTransitionPendingIntent();
    createGeofences();
    Log.i(TAG, "Adding geofences to API location services");
     LocationServices.GeofencingApi.addGeofences(mGoogleApiClient,
geofenceList,mGeofencePendingIntent);      }
}

private PendingIntent getGeofenceTransitionPendingIntent()
{
  Intent intent = new Intent(this,
GeofenceTransitionsIntentService.class);
  return PendingIntent.getService(this, 0, intent,
PendingIntent.FLAG_UPDATE_CURRENT);
}

@Override public void onConnectionSuspended(int i)
{
  Log.i(TAG, "onConnectionSuspended called");
}

@Override public void onConnectionFailed(@NonNull ConnectionResult
connectionResult)
{
  Log.i(TAG, "onConnectionFailed called");      }
}
```

Note that the `SimpleGeofence` class we use takes three arguments; it internally sets the radius to 50 meters. See the sample code on GitHub for more implementation details.

To-do list view

The following figure depicts what the to-do list view looks like. Users can add to-do items, and delete existing ones. Each item in the list is displayed, along with its location:

Adding to-do items

The following image shows sample input for adding a new to-do item to the `Today-Todo` app:

Mock locations

You may have noticed that we chose to define two locations–home and work. Now, because we have high aspirations, we have ventured to build this app with the most deserving individual in mind, namely the President of the United States. So, that is why the home coordinates correspond to that of the White House, and the work coordinates correspond to that of Capitol Hill (Okay, bad example, we know. The President works in the Oval office in the west wing of the White House complex. But then, imagine how pointless our sample code would be if `Work` and `Home` had the same coordinates?). The `Constants` file with these values is shown in the following figure:

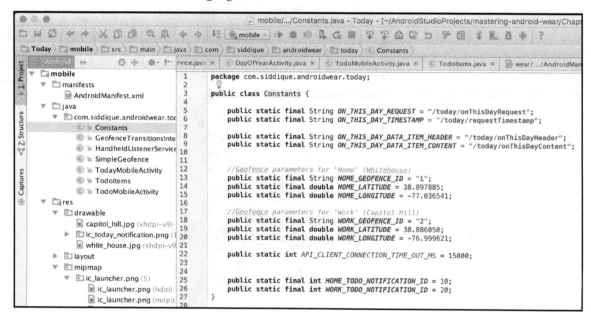

Mocking locations using FakeGPS app

Launch the FakeGPS app and search for the location White House as follows:

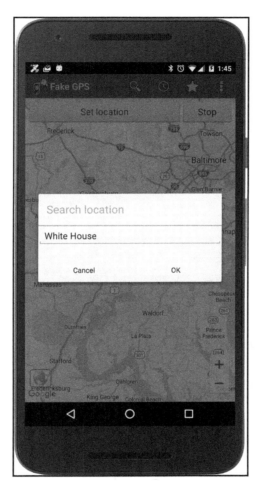

After you tap the **Set location** button, FakeGPS will proceed to simulate the location we set. Take note of the latitude and longitude in the preceding figure. See how close they are to what we defined in `Constants.HOME_LATITUDE` and `Constants.HOME_LONGITUDE` in the `Constant` file:

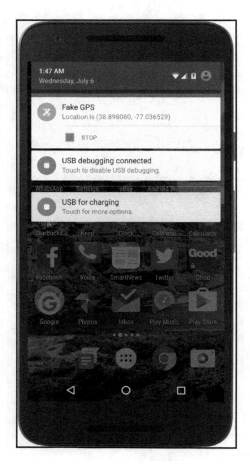

The GeofenceTransitionIntentService class

You may recall from the `TodoMobileActivity` activity, which we covered previously, that the `GeofenceIntentService` class will be called anytime there are changes in location. The `onHandleIntent` method is where we place code that will notify the user about any to-do items based on the `geofence` location that the user may have entered:

```
public class GeofenceTransitionsIntentService extends IntentService
```

```
{
  private static final String TAG =
GeofenceTransitionsIntentService.class.getName();

  public GeofenceTransitionsIntentService()
  {
    super(GeofenceTransitionsIntentService.class.getSimpleName());
  }

  @Override
  public void onCreate()
  {
    super.onCreate();
  }
  /*
  *Handles incoming intents.*
  * @param intent The Intent sent by Location Services. This Intent is
provided to Location
  *Services (inside a PendingIntent) when addGeofences() is called.
  */
  @Override
  protected void onHandleIntent(Intent intent)
  {
    Log.i(TAG, "Location changed " + intent);
    GeofencingEvent geoFenceEvent =  GeofencingEvent.fromIntent(intent);
    if (geoFenceEvent.hasError())
    {
      int errorCode = geoFenceEvent.getErrorCode();
      Log.e(TAG, "Location Services error: " + errorCode);
    }
    else
    {
      int transitionType = geoFenceEvent.getGeofenceTransition();
      // Get an instance of the NotificationManager service
      NotificationManagerCompat notificationManager =
NotificationManagerCompat.from(this);

    Log.i(TAG, "Notifying home todo items");
    String triggeredGeoFenceId =
geoFenceEvent.getTriggeringGeofences().get(0)
      .getRequestId();
    switch (triggeredGeoFenceId)
    {
      case Constants.HOME_GEOFENCE_ID:
      if (Geofence.GEOFENCE_TRANSITION_ENTER == transitionType)
      {
        Log.i(TAG, "Notifying home todo items");
        notifyTodoItems(notificationManager, "Home",
```

```
Constants.HOME_TODO_NOTIFICATION_ID, R.drawable.white_house);
      }
    break;

    case Constants.WORK_GEOFENCE_ID:
      if (Geofence.GEOFENCE_TRANSITION_ENTER == transitionType)
      {
        Log.i(TAG, "Notifying work todo items");
        notifyTodoItems(notificationManager, "Work",
Constants.WORK_TODO_NOTIFICATION_ID, R.drawable.capitol_hill);
      }
      break;
    }
  }
}

  private void notifyTodoItems(NotificationManagerCompat
notificationManager, String todoItemType, int notificationId, int
background)
{
  Set<String> todoItems = TodoItems.readItems(this, todoItemType);
  Intent viewIntent = new Intent(this, TodoMobileActivity.class);
  PendingIntent viewPendingIntent = PendingIntent.getActivity(this, 0,
viewIntent,  PendingIntent.FLAG_UPDATE_CURRENT);

  NotificationCompat.Builder notificationBuilder = new
NotificationCompat.Builder(this)
  .setSmallIcon(R.drawable.ic_today_notification)
  .setLargeIcon(BitmapFactory.decodeResource(
  getResources(), background))
  .setContentTitle(todoItems.size() + " " + todoItemType + " todo  items
found!")   .setContentText(todoItems.toString()     )
  .setContentIntent(viewPendingIntent);

// Build the notification and issues it with notification manager.
  notificationManager.notify(notificationId,  notificationBuilder.build());
  }
}
```

Handheld app notification

The following figure shows a run of the application with FakeGPS app set to Home. See the notification display on the handheld device showing three to-do items tied to the Home location:

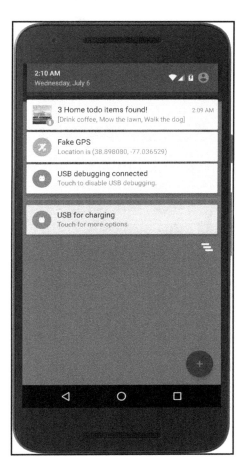

Wearable app notifications

The following figure shows the same notification on the wearable device:

Now, if we change the location in the FakeGPS app to `Capitol Hill` and relaunch the `Today-Todo` app, we get a different notification, as expected, in the wearable device, as shown in the following screenshot:

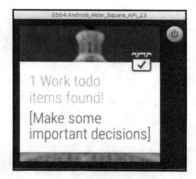

Summary

In this chapter, we extended the `Today` app to have a to-do activity. We use that extension to demonstrate context-aware notifications using the `Notifications` API. The notifications were displayed on the mobile device as well as the wearable device emulator. We introduced the concept of geofencing and used the `Geofencing` API along with a FakeGPS app to simulate our location.

7
Voice Interactions, Sensors, and Tracking

"All I have is a voice."
– W. H. Auden

In this chapter, we cover the voice capabilities offered by the Wear API and define voice actions interfacing with our Today app from the previous chapter. We also introduce device sensors and discuss how they can be used to track data.

 The code accompanying this chapter is available for reference on GitHub (https://github.com/siddii/mastering-android-wear/tree/master /Chapter_7). For the sake of brevity, only code snippets are included as needed. The reader is encouraged to download the referenced code from GitHub and follow along as they progress through the chapter.

Voice capabilities

If you lived your adolescence through the eighties, chances are you got all your knowledge of wearable device voice interactions from this guy:

Three decades on, here you are, itching to find out whether the `Wear` API offers a system-provided voice action that enables you to summon your car. I'm afraid, not yet. The complete list of system-provided voice actions is presented in the subsection that follows.

 You can visit the Android's developer site (`https://developer.android.com/training/wearables/apps/voice.html`) for more insight on the voice capabilities for your wearable app.

By system-provided voice actions, we mean the voice actions that are built into the Wear platform, that is, provided out of the box for developer use.

In contrast, the term app-provided voice actions refer to those that are specific to your app.

System-provided voice actions

System-provided voice actions must be filtered according to the specific activity you want to start when the phrase corresponding to the voice action is spoken. For instance, note to self.

The Wear platform supports the following voice intents:

- Take a note
- Call a car/taxi
- Set alarm
- Set timer
- Start/stop a run
- Start/stop a bike ride
- Start stopwatch
- Start/stop a run
- Start/stop a workout
- Show step count
- Show heart rate

App-provided voice actions

Depending on your needs, the system-provided voice actions may not be enough. In that case, you can choose to register a start action for your app the same way you register a launcher icon on a handheld.

To start `TodayActivity` using a voice action, specify a label attribute with a text value set to whatever you say after the `Start` keyword. In this sample code, we use our app name as the label attribute. The existence of an intent-filter tag recognizes the voice action `Start Today` and launches the `TodayActivity` activity:

```
<activity
  android:name=".TodayActivity"
  android:label="@string/app_name">
  <intent-filter>
    <action android:name="android.intent.action.MAIN" />
    <category android:name="android.intent.category.LAUNCHER" />
  </intent-filter>
</activity>
```

New feature – adding to-do items through voice commands

Let's get ready to write some code. In the last chapter, we augmented our `Today` app to allow us to add to-do items through a paired handheld app. The wearable then surfaced notifications based on configured contexts.

Now, let's spice that up by adding voice interactions to the mix. We'll use the wearable app to take to-do notes through voice commands. This will involve extending the context-aware notifications feature we implemented with the ability to add to-do items using voice inputs. Furthermore, we will supply the context along with the to-do item.

For example, if we were to say "home make dinner", our wearable app will create a to-do item named *Make dinner* and associate it with the `Home` context. In the same way, if we were to say "work set up monthly review meeting", the app will create a to-do item named *Set up monthly review meeting* and associate it with the `Work` context.

A few things to keep in mind before we step through the code:

- At the time of this writing, Android Wear emulators do not support voice inputs. So we opted to use a physical wear device.
- Now, if you recall, we had mentioned previously that we don't really need a physical device to build Android Wear apps. While that is true for the most part, there are cases where the emulators cannot emulate physical device behaviors such as voice inputs, motion sensing, and so on. In these cases, we really have no option besides getting hold of a physical device for a fuller Android wear development experience. Besides, if you're serious about Android Wear development, you might as well consider getting a physical device because it really helps speed up your development.
- It is important to note that while voice interactions are not presently supported in Android Wear emulators, Google might up their support for voice interactions in the future. We'll be keeping an eye on that.

Add to-do Item – a new action in the wearable app

Let's get started. One of the first things we will do is add an `Add Todo Item` action to our `arrays.xml` file:

```xml
<?xml version="1.0" encoding="utf-8"?>
<resources>
  <string-array name="actions">
    <item>Day of Year</item>
    <item>On this day...</item>
    <item>Add Todo Item</item>
  </string-array>
</resources>
```

This newly configured action is now displayed on our screen, as shown here:

The AddTodoItem activity in the wearable app

We wire in the handler for the selection of the `AddTodoItem` activity:

```java
@Override
public void onClick(WearableListView.ViewHolder viewHolder)
```

```
    {
      Log.i(TAG, "Clicked list item" + viewHolder.getAdapterPosition());
      if (viewHolder.getAdapterPosition() == 0)
      {
        Intent intent = new Intent(this, DayOfYearActivity.class);
        startActivity(intent);
      }
      else if (viewHolder.getAdapterPosition() == 1)
      {
        Intent intent = new Intent(this, OnThisDayActivity.class);
        startActivity(intent);
      }
      else if (viewHolder.getAdapterPosition() == 2)
      {
        displaySpeechRecognizer();
      }

    //Create an intent that can start the Speech Recognizer activity
    private void displaySpeechRecognizer()
    {
      Intent intent = new  Intent(RecognizerIntent.ACTION_RECOGNIZE_SPEECH);
      intent.putExtra(RecognizerIntent.EXTRA_LANGUAGE_MODEL,
      RecognizerIntent.LANGUAGE_MODEL_FREE_FORM);
      // Start the activity, the intent will be populated with the speech text
      startActivityForResult(intent, Constants.SPEECH_REQUEST_CODE);
    }
```

Clicking on the **Add Todo Item** action has the following effect:

Handling speech inputs

The `onActivityResult` method callback fires when the speech recognizer returns with the voice input intent. Note how we extract the spoken text and then call the `GoogleApiClient` API if the voice command begins with one of our predefined contexts, namely `home` or `work`:

```java
// This callback is invoked when the Speech Recognizer returns.
// This is where you process the intent and extract the speech text from
the intent.
@Override
protected void onActivityResult(int requestCode, int resultCode,  Intent
data)
{
   if (requestCode == Constants.SPEECH_REQUEST_CODE && resultCode   ==
RESULT_OK)
   {
     List<String> results = data.getStringArrayListExtra(
RecognizerIntent.EXTRA_RESULTS);
     spokenText = results.get(0);
     // Do something with spokenText
     Log.i(TAG, "Spoken Text = " + spokenText);
     if (spokenText.startsWith("home") ||  spokenText.startsWith("work"))
     {
       Log.i(TAG, "Creating Google Api Client");
       mGoogleApiClient = new GoogleApiClient.Builder(this)
       addApi(Wearable.API)
       .addConnectionCallbacks(this)
       .addOnConnectionFailedListener(this)
       .build();
        mGoogleApiClient.connect();
     }
   }
   else
   {
     super.onActivityResult(requestCode,  resultCode, data);
   }
}
```

Android Wear parses the speech input and presents the spoken text as a confirmation, as shown here:

Once `GoogleClient` is connected, that is, the `onConnected` handler fires, we extract the `todoItem` text after excluding the context (`home` or `work`) and send the to-do item as a message to the handheld app using the `Wearable Data` API:

```
@Override
public void onConnected(Bundle bundle)
{
  Log.i(TAG, "Connected to Data Api");
  if(spokenText != null)
  {
    if (spokenText.startsWith("home"))
    {
      String todoItem = spokenText.substring("home".length());
      sendMessage(Constants.HOME_TODO_ITEM, todoItem.getBytes());
    }
    else if(spokenText.startsWith("work"))
    {
      String todoItem = spokenText.substring("work".length());
      sendMessage(Constants.WORK_TODO_ITEM, todoItem.getBytes());
    }
  }
}

private void sendMessage(final String path, final byte[] data)
{
```

```
Log.i(TAG, "Sending message to path " + path);
Wearable.NodeApi.getConnectedNodes(mGoogleApiClient).setResultCallback(
new ResultCallback<NodeApi.GetConnectedNodesResult>()
{
  @Override
  public void onResult(NodeApi.GetConnectedNodesResult nodes)
  {
    for (Node node : nodes.getNodes())
    {
      Wearable.MessageApi
      sendMessage(mGoogleApiClient, node.getId(), path, data);
      spokenText = null;
    }
  }
});
}
```

Handheld app

Over on the handheld app, we implement the `onMessageReceived` handler to process the message received from the wearable. Remember, the handheld app is where we do the heavy-lifting work. In this case, it is the creation of a to-do item:

```
@Override
public void onMessageReceived(MessageEvent messageEvent)
{
  super.onMessageReceived(messageEvent);
  Log.i(TAG, "Message received" + messageEvent);
  if(Constants.ON_THIS_DAY_REQUEST.equals(messageEvent.getPath()))
  {
    //read Today's content from Wikipedia
    getOnThisDayContentFromWikipedia();
  }
  else
  {
    String todo = new String(messageEvent.getData());
    if (Constants.HOME_TODO_ITEM.equals(messageEvent.getPath()))
    {
      Log.i(TAG, "Adding home todo item '" + todo + "'");
      TodoItems.addItem(this, "Home", todo);
    }
    else if (Constants.WORK_TODO_ITEM.equals(messageEvent.getPath()))
    {
      Log.i(TAG, "Adding work todo item '" + todo + "'");
      TodoItems.addItem(this, "Work", todo);        }
  }
```

```
    }
```

The added to-do item is displayed in the to-do list on our handheld's `Today - Todos` app, as shown here:

Motion sensors

Motion sensors let us monitor the motion of a device through space, such as a rotation, swing, shake, or tilt. The movement may be relative to its immediate environment as is the case when you mimic a steering wheel in a car simulation. In this case, we monitor its motion relative to its own frame of reference or that of the application running on it.

However, the movement may also be relative to the environment surrounding the device, namely the world. An example of the latter is determining absolute speed from inside a moving vehicle. The device may be stationary inside the vehicle, but it is moving with respect to the earth at the same speed as the vehicle itself.

The Android platform lets us monitor the motion of a device using a broad array of sensors–some are hardware-based, such as the gyroscope and accelerometer. Others are software-based or they may be hardware-based but dependent on other hardware sensors. Examples are the rotation vector sensor, the gravity sensor, the significant motion sensor, the step counter sensor and the step detector sensor. You can read all about these on the developers site (`https://developer.android.com/guide/topics/sensors/sensors_moti on.html`).

Our concern in this section is to provide a very brief treatment of two hardware sensors that are at the very heart of all motion sensing the gyroscope and the accelerometer. Understanding the principles underlying these sensors will give us an appreciation for the physics that pervades the behavior of all motion sensors and will leave us with an intuitive sense of how to go about solving our application problems through the indirect use of these sensors via the API available to us.

Gyroscope

A gyroscope (jÄ«roË®skÅ®p) is, at its most basic level, a device consisting of a wheel or disk mounted so that it can spin freely about an axis without being influenced by the orientation of the mount that encloses it.

The following image helps us better visualize the construction:

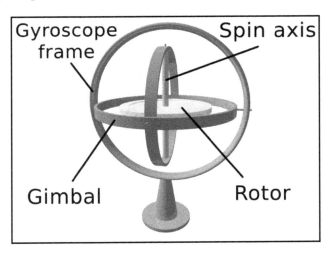

For the purposes of gaining an intuitive understanding, we just need to digest the fact that the properties of a gyroscope are only manifested while the rotor (disk) is rotating about its axis. When the disk is not rotating, the device does not exhibit any useful properties. But when rotating, the orientation of this axis is unaffected by the tilting or rotation of the mounting. This is in accordance with the conservation of angular momentum, and in essence, this is what makes a gyroscope useful for measuring or maintaining orientation.

Accelerometer

An accelerometer is an instrument for measuring acceleration, typically that of an automobile, ship, aircraft, or spacecraft, or that involved in the vibration of a machine, building, or other structure.

Accelerometers find application in many fields of science and industry. For example, accelerometers are used to detect and monitor vibrations in rotating machinery. They are also used in tablets and digital cameras to ensure that images are always displayed upright on screen.

In the domain of wear devices, an acceleration sensor measures the acceleration applied to the device, which includes the forces of gravity. In general, the accelerometer is typically a good choice if you are monitoring device motion. It is available in almost every Android-powered handheld and tablet. It consumes significantly less power than the other motion sensors.

New feature – tracking our steps

Everyone loves step counters. How about we build one for our wearable device? Not much to talk about here, so let's dive into the code.

Add to-do item – a new action in the wearable app

The first thing we will do here is to add a menu `item` to the wearable app. Let's call it `Step Count`. Our changes to `arrays.xml` file would be as follows:

```xml
<?xml version="1.0" encoding="utf-8"?>
<resources>
    <string-array name="actions">
        <item>Day of Year</item>
        <item>On this day...</item>
        <item>Add Todo Item</item>
        <item>Step Count</item>
    </string-array>
</resources>
```

This action should now show up on the wearable app, as shown in the following figure:

Click on the Step Count menu item to launch the corresponding StepCounterActivity activity. The code for that class is given here. Note how the activity implements the SensorEventListener class. We hook up the correct sensor type using the SensorManager class in the onCreate handler for this activity. Take note of the other handlers you would expect this activity to be associated with owing to its implementation of the SensorEventListener class:

```java
public class StepCounterActivity extends Activity implements
SensorEventListener
{
    private SensorManager mSensorManager;
    private Sensor mSensor;

    // Steps counted since the last reboot
    private int mSteps = 0;

    private static final String TAG =  StepCounterActivity.class.getName();

    @Override
    protected void onCreate(Bundle savedInstanceState)
    {
        super.onCreate(savedInstanceState);
        setContentView(R.layout.activity_daily_step_counter);

        mSensorManager = (SensorManager)
getSystemService(Context.SENSOR_SERVICE);
```

```java
    mSensor = mSensorManager.getDefaultSensor(Sensor.TYPE_STEP_COUNTER);
}

@Override
protected void onResume()
{
  super.onResume();
  mSensorManager.registerListener(this, mSensor,
SensorManager.SENSOR_DELAY_NORMAL);
  refreshStepCount();
}

@Override
protected void onPause()
{
  super.onPause();
  mSensorManager.unregisterListener(this);
}

@Override
public void onSensorChanged(SensorEvent event)
{
  Log.i(TAG,"onSensorChanged - " + event.values[0]);
  if(event.sensor.getType() == Sensor.TYPE_STEP_COUNTER)
  {
    Log.i(TAG,"Total step count: " + mSteps);
    mSteps = (int) event.values[0];
    refreshStepCount();
  }
}
private void refreshStepCount()
{
  TextView desc = (TextView)  findViewById(R.id.daily_step_count_desc);
  desc.setText(getString(R.string.daily_step_count_desc,  mSteps));
}

@Override
public void onAccuracyChanged(Sensor sensor, int accuracy)
{
  Log.i(TAG,"onAccuracyChanged - " + sensor);
}
}
```

This is how our new activity appears on the wearable device:

As shown in the preceding code, the type of sensor we use here is denoted by the `TYPE_STEP_COUNTER` constant of the `Sensor` class. This type of sensor gets the number of steps that the user has taken since the last reboot of the wearable device. The important thing to remember about this sensor type is that applications need to stay registered because the step counter does not track steps if it is not activated.

We chose this basic type of sensor because our focus was on using the API. Feel free to explore the `Sensor` API class here to study the other sensors available to you. In particular, take a look at the `TYPE_STEP_DETECTOR` sensor type. This one triggers an event every time the user takes a step. Unlike the step counter, which tracks steps taken over a period of time, the step detector is ideal for detecting a step at the very moment it is taken.

You can also think about how you would go about implementing a step counter for a given day–an exercise left to the interested reader who wants to make the most of our `Today` app.

Summary

In this chapter, we demonstrated the creation of app-provided voice actions using the `Wear` API to launch our `Today Todo` app. We also introduced motion sensor concepts and examined the API classes that let us avail of these sensors. We then applied these concepts to augment our sample `Today` application with a simple activity that tracks the number of steps a user has taken.

8
Creating Custom UI

"I have said that she had no face, but that meant she had a thousand faces."
                                                                  - C. S. Lewis

In this chapter, we will cover the design principles that are central to the Android Wear UI spaces and go over a few common Wear UI patterns. We then extend the `OnThisDay` activity to present the feed in a user-friendly format.

 The code accompanying this chapter is available for reference on GitHub (`https://github.com/siddii/mastering-android-wear/tree/master /Chapter_8`). For the sake of brevity, only code snippets are included as needed. The reader is encouraged to download the referenced code from GitHub and follow along as they progress through the chapter.

Android Wear UI design

By now, it should be clear to us that wearable apps cannot always follow the same UI patterns that their handheld counterparts might. Wearable devices have a significantly smaller form factor and interacting with them places heavier constraints on user actions. For this reason, the Android Wear user interface APIs are functionally divided into *Suggest* functions and *Demand* functions.

The *Suggest* functions are embodied by the `Context` stream—a stream of information presented in a manner that is proactive and suggestive. Users are shown a vertical list of informational cards, which can be scrolled through until the user wishes to interact with a specific card.

The *Demand* functions are reflected in the cue card metaphor. A cue card can be opened by saying **OK Google**, or, we can open it by tapping on the background of the home screen. Each voice command activates a type of voice intent, which in turn can be associated with multiple applications.

When presented with intent, the user will have the opportunity to choose which application they would like the intent activated for. Applications can respond by adding/updating a stream card or launching another application.

Common UI patterns

We will touch upon the most commonly implemented UI patterns in Android Wear development.

Cards

The cards that are displayed in the Context stream can be standard notifications, single-action cards, or an expandable stack that groups related notifications together. In each case, an icon located at the top-right edge of the card indicates the application that the card is associated with.

In some cases, a single notification card does not suffice and more details may be needed. A swipe from right to left can reveal detail cards in addition to the main Context stream card. A swipe from left to right on a card causes it to be removed from the Context stream.

It is noteworthy that notifications dismissed on the wearable will cause them to be dismissed on a paired handheld as well due to the synchronized state shared by paired devices.

A card can optionally display action buttons to the right of detail cards. These actions may run on the wearable itself. Alternatively, they may be delegated to the companion handheld or they can cause a full-screen activity to run.

Countdowns and confirmations

When a user taps on an action button shown to the right of a detail card, the system can display a confirmation animation when the action completes.

In some cases, it may be desired to give the user a chance to interrupt an action before it executes. One way to address this is to display a customizable countdown animation prior to the action invocation.

Some actions may be critical in nature and it may be desired to highlight this by showing the user a confirmation step. The user would then have to confirm their intention to execute the action.

As developers, we should always weigh the option to delegate any heavy lifting work to the companion handheld whenever it is possible to do so. If this is the case for an action invoked on a card in the Context stream, then we may choose to display an animation on the wearable once the action button has been tapped by the user and the corresponding app has been launched on the handheld device.

There is also the option to have on-card actions. These are actions that execute on the card itself. These are ideal when there is only one possible action that a tap can have. For instance, a car icon displaying on a notification showing an address can only imply directions and is thus a good candidate to be an on-card action. An on-card action should be unambiguous in its purpose.

The alternative (that is, when there are multiple possible actions) is to invoke them via action buttons to the right of a detail card. For instance, in the case of a person's name, an on-card action is ambiguous, so separate action buttons would work better, for example, for actions such as call, e-mail, show details, and so on.

Card stacks

Some cards may be related and it makes sense to group them together in a stack. For instance, to display new mail notifications, a card stack can group all new mail notifications together.

Users would click on the card stack to make it fan out and display the top edge of each card in the stack. Further tapping on a fanned-out card will open the card to its fully expanded state in the vertical list that is the Context stream.

When the user swipes vertically away from a card stack, all the cards in the stack return to their fully collapsed state and the singular stack displays again in the Context stream.

2D Pickers

The 2D Picker is a flexible UI pattern used in Android Wear apps. It allows us to build one-dimensional lists of cards or two-dimensional grids of cards, as dictated by requirements.

Furthermore, the direction of the scroll can be set as either horizontal or vertical. Data presented to the user is distributed across pages, and each page then corresponds to a card.

One intuitive presentation is to display a vertical list of cards to the user comprising (say) results of a search. Each card in the vertical list presents a small amount of information, and more information can be obtained by scrolling horizontally from it to display subsequent cards containing the remaining pages of information.

The 2D Picker pattern is implemented by adding an instance of a `GridViewPager` element to the layout of the activity in question. This pager must then have an adapter set for it of the `GridPagerAdapter` type.

To make things simpler, an abstract class extending the `GridPageAdapter` class named `FragmentGridPageAdapter` defines the common behavior your adapter will need, so all you have to do is extend the `FragmentGridPageAdapter` class to implement your own adapter to provide a set of pages to populate the `GridViewPager` element with.

When using a 2D Picker presentation, we must ensure that we optimize it to get the speed. This can be done by keeping the cards simple and minimizing the number of cards in the picker.

The 2D Picker should be destroyed when the user makes a selection. Users may also initiate an exit from a 2D picker by swiping down on the first card or swiping right on a left-most card.

Selection lists

This is a common pattern whereby possible choices are presented in a simple scrollable list. Users select an item from the list and thereby invoke an action.

The Android Wear UI library provides an implementation of a list that is optimized for wearables, namely the `WearableListView` element. To create a list of this kind, you add a `WearableListView` element to your activity's layout definition and then set its adapter to an instance of your custom layout implementation.

Revisiting the OnThisDay activity

Note that our initial implementation of the `OnThisDayActivity` activity from Chapter 5, *Synchronizing Data*, utilized a `TextView` method within a `ScrollView` method. Let's spruce that up using a few simple UI patterns we introduced in this chapter. We will intentionally keep this code simple to give you a chance to grasp the new API classes we use. You are encouraged to contrive use cases and experiment with more interesting patterns such as the 2D Picker.

Enough talk. It's time to write some code. We're now ready to improve our initial *On this day* feed presentation with a vertical list comprising cards. Each card can be dismissed by a swipe from left to right. The result is a far more usable application.

The OnThisDayActivity activity

The following `showOnThisDay` method creates and sets up a `GridViewPager` instance that properly handles the layout depending on the display:

```
private void showOnThisDay(OnThisDay onThisDay)
{
   final Resources res = getResources();
   final GridViewPager pager = (GridViewPager) findViewById(R.id.pager);
   pager.setOnApplyWindowInsetsListener(new
View.OnApplyWindowInsetsListener()
   {
      @Override
      public WindowInsets onApplyWindowInsets(View v, WindowInsets insets)
      {
         // Adjust page margins:
         // A little extra horizontal spacing between pages looks a bit
         // less crowded on a round display.

         final boolean round = insets.isRound();
         int rowMargin = res.getDimensionPixelOffset(R.dimen.page_row_margin);
         int colMargin = res.getDimensionPixelOffset(round ?
R.dimen.page_column_margin_round : R.dimen.page_column_margin);
         pager.setPageMargins(rowMargin, colMargin);
         // GridViewPager relies on insets to properly handle
         // layout for round displays. They must be explicitly
         // applied since this listener has taken them over.
         pager.onApplyWindowInsets(insets);
         return insets;
      }
   });
```

```
    pager.setAdapter(new OnThisDayGridPagerAdapter(this,
getFragmentManager(), onThisDay));
    DotsPageIndicator dotsPageIndicator = (DotsPageIndicator)
findViewById(R.id.page_indicator);
    DotsPageIndicator.setPager(pager);
}
```

The `DotsPageIndicator` is a page indicator for the `GridViewPager` class that helps to identify the current page with respect to the available pages on the current row. Dots represent pages; the current page can be distinguished by a dot of a distinct color and/or size.

The activity layout

The following activity layout shows the declaration of a `GridViewPager` element where previously (in `Chapter 5`, *Synchronizing Data*) we had a `TextView` method within a `ScrollView` method:

```xml
<android.support.wearable.view.BoxInsetLayout
xmlns:android="http://schemas.android.com/apk/res/android"
    xmlns:app="http://schemas.android.com/apk/res-auto"
    android:layout_width="match_parent"
    android:layout_height="match_parent"
    android:background="@color/yellow_orange">

    <FrameLayout xmlns:android="http://schemas.android.com/apk/res/android"
        android:layout_width="match_parent"
        android:layout_height="match_parent" >

        <android.support.wearable.view.GridViewPager
            android:id="@+id/pager"
            android:layout_width="match_parent"
            android:layout_height="match_parent"
            android:keepScreenOn="true" />

        <android.support.wearable.view.DotsPageIndicator
            android:id="@+id/page_indicator"
            android:layout_width="wrap_content"
            android:layout_height="wrap_content"
            android:layout_gravity="center_horizontal|bottom">
        </android.support.wearable.view.DotsPageIndicator>
    </FrameLayout>
</android.support.wearable.view.BoxInsetLayout>
```

We define an `OnThisDayGridPagerAdapter` class extending the `FragmentGridPagerAdapter` class. An instance of this class is set as the adapter attribute of the `GridViewPager` element. A private inner class named `Row` is used as a convenience container for Fragment objects:

```
public class OnThisDayGridPagerAdapter extends FragmentGridPagerAdapter
{
  private final Context mContext;
  private OnThisDay onThisDay;
  private List<Row> mRows;
  private ColorDrawable mDefaultBg;
  private ColorDrawable mClearBg;
  public OnThisDayGridPagerAdapter(Context ctx, FragmentManager fm,
OnThisDay onThisDay)
  {
    super(fm);
    mContext = ctx;
    this.onThisDay = onThisDay;
    mRows = new ArrayList<OnThisDayGridPagerAdapter.Row>();
    ArrayList<String> listItems = onThisDay.getListItems();
    for (String listItem: listItems)
    {
      mRows.add(new Row(cardFragment("On This Day - " +
(listItems.indexOf(listItem) + 1), listItem)));
    }
  }
  private Fragment cardFragment(String title, String content)
  {
    Resources res = mContext.getResources();
    CardFragment fragment = CardFragment.create(title, content);
    // Add some extra bottom margin to leave room for the page indicator
    fragment.setCardMarginBottom(
res.getDimensionPixelSize(R.dimen.card_margin_bottom));
    return fragment;
  }
  /** A convenient container for a row of fragments. */
  private class Row
  {
    final List<Fragment> columns = new ArrayList<Fragment>();
    public Row(Fragment... fragments)
    {
      for (Fragment f : fragments)
      {
        add(f);
      }
    }
    public void add(Fragment f)
```

```
      {
        columns.add(f);
      }
      Fragment getColumn(int i)
      {
        return columns.get(i);
      }
      public int getColumnCount()
      {
        return columns.size();
      }
    }
    @Override
    public Fragment getFragment(int row, int col)
    {
      Row adapterRow = mRows.get(row);
      return adapterRow.getColumn(col);
    }

    @Override
    public Drawable getBackgroundForRow(final int row)
    {
      return mContext.getResources().getDrawable(R.drawable.page_background);
    }

    @Override
    public int getRowCount()
    {
      return mRows.size();
    }

    @Override
    public int getColumnCount(int rowNum)
    {
      return mRows.get(rowNum).getColumnCount();
    }
  }
```

We run the application and choose the **On this day...** activity, as shown in the following screenshot:

Each item from the feed result is now presented as a card in a scrollable vertical list, as shown in the following screenshot:

You can take a look at the second example by just scrolling vertically:

Summary

In this chapter, we went over Android Wear design principles and surveyed the common UI patterns that the majority of wearable applications implement. We then put the API to use by writing some code to augment the **On this day...** activity of the Today app from Chapter 5, *Synchronizing Data*, with a GridViewPager component that displays a list of cards and lets the user interact with them.

9
Material Design

"This world is but a canvas to our imagination."
— Henry David Thoreau

In this chapter, we provide a conceptual understanding of material design and touch upon a few key principles specific to wearable app design and development. We solidify our understanding by extending our `Todo` app from previous chapters to incorporate a navigation drawer that lets us switch between `Todo` categories and view items and perform actions specific to each category.

 The code accompanying this chapter is available for reference on GitHub (`https://github.com/siddii/mastering-android-wear/tree/master /Chapter_9`). For the sake of brevity, only code snippets are included as needed. The reader is encouraged to download the referenced code from GitHub and follow along as they progress through the chapter.

Approaching material design

Your primary resource to understanding material design is `material.google.com`, which is the living online documentation outlining the tenets and principles of material design. It really ought to be bookmarked by any serious designer or developer enthused by material design.

While we encourage you to read through Google's documentation, we feel that it would not be terribly superfluous if we advanced an approach on how to think about material design. Our goal is to give you, as a reader interested in the material design philosophy, an intuitive and symbolic understanding of the paradigm. We hope that this brief introduction readies you with a mindset that will expedite your journey through the material design online documentation and stimulate a level of creativity that should leave you well-positioned to project your imagination onto tangible design ideas for your wearable apps.

This section is only intended for those of us who may be new to the idea and may need a primer that is hopefully sufficient to light a spark and get us thinking anew.

Interacting with the world

We can go over a formal definition of material design, maybe even more than one. But, that would not be a good use of our time. Google's documentation does a great job at that and more. Rather than getting caught up in articulations of what material design is, let's step back and understand what exactly the motivation behind it is.

For our purposes, let us consider the scenario where you are at a coffee shop, sitting at a table. Take a look at the empty tabletop in the following figure:

Your tabletop has great potential to become your workspace. Let's call that potential **affordance**. The term affordance generally means a possibility of an action of an object or environment. For instance, looking at a steering wheel of a car, it is natural to think that it should be rotated to make it operational rather than pulled or pushed.

Let's spend a moment and study our workspace:

- It is flat
- It has clear boundaries; in this case, the continuous edge of the circle that defines the shape of our table
- In its initial state, it holds no objects

Let's stop there and interact with our table a little bit. Here we go:

Now our table is not empty anymore. Let's continue with our observations:

- Objects that get on the table, stay on the table; they don't slide off by themselves, nor do they float away (thank you, gravity).
- Objects can be moved on the table subject to its bounds.
- Only objects that we care about are on the table. Objects that we don't care about, we tend to take them off the table. Do you see my notepad on there? Not yet, because I haven't cared about it enough.

Let's change this:

Okay, this is starting to look a bit more familiar now. Here are some more observations:

- Objects share space if they need to be readily accessible.
- When an object has my attention, it is on top.
- At any given time, each object on the table occupies a specific (how should I say it) elevation depending on whether it is on top of everything else, at the bottom (that is, directly on the table), or between other objects.
- As the number of objects on the table increases, the affordance can increase. Affordance is a term used in **Human Computer Interaction** (**HCI**) to describe the possible actions a user can take while interacting with the objects.

We can go on and on, making all sorts of intelligent observations about what is possible and what isn't with respect to our surface (the table) and the objects on it. What's important, however, is that all of these observations are completely unnecessary to our successful use of the table and the heap of objects we pile on to it to help us get through all our work, or play, as the case may be.

The reasons for this are likely more suited to a talk on HCI or more broadly, the fields of perceptive/cognitive/environmental psychology. All we need to understand and appreciate is that our intuitive understanding of how we use surfaces and interact with them can hold the key to a productive and efficient design of user interfaces.

A visual language

The question to ask is how does all this help us design better user interfaces?

The designers at Google have distilled our knowledge of, and experience with, how we interact with surfaces in the real world into a set of tenets and principles collectively referred to as **Material Design**. These tenets and principles are laid out at `material.google.com`, which should be our primary reference for all things material design.

What do we mean by the term material?
It is worth clarifying that when Google documentation uses the term *material*, it is essentially used to refer to any of the graphical objects in your visual design. These may be navigational objects, action bars, dialogs, and so on. Each material object you can interact with has dimensions (height and width), it is of a standard thickness, and it is located on an imaginary surface at a specific elevation (along the z-axis) in the three-dimensional space of the view in question.

To equip ourselves with an understanding of what material design is, it is required that we adopt a mindset necessary to material design thinking. Of course, the way we interact with the real world does not always translate directly to the way we interact with devices. But where there is an overlap, it must be exploited to employ the user's intuitive powers to further the usability of the system. Where our interaction with the real world is quite limited, software enriches the user experience by expanding the realm of possibilities to surpass that of the physical world, while at all times respecting and engaging user intuition.

As you read through the precepts at `material.google.com`, you will come across detailed discussions of the following, to cite a few:

- The idea of material inspired by paper and ink
- Key light and ambient light as visual cues to elevation (shadow size and sharpness)
- The motion respects the user as the prime initiator of movement
- Each material object has three dimensions (*x*, *y*, and *z* coordinates) and always occupies a fixed z-axis position
- Objects are presented to the user as seamlessly as possible
- The rules of physics are respected
- When the rules are broken, they are broken intentionally, for instance, to capture the user's attention
- How objects can and should be manipulated and how they should not be

- Material motion and transformation
- Core iconography and typography
- Navigational components and patterns

The adoption of material design philosophy in our design and development practices becomes even more important when working with apps for wearable devices where the form factor is decreased significantly, thereby increasing our usability challenges. Building upon these widely recognized metaphors is key to ensuring the usability and longevity of our wearable apps.

Now, let's write some code.

To-do item menus

Let's augment the `Today Todo` app with a powerful design metaphor–*navigation drawers*.

The first thing we need to do is add a `Todos` action to our `arrays.xml` file, as follows:

```xml
<?xml version="1.0" encoding="utf-8"?>
<resources>
  <string-array name="actions">
    <item>Day of Year</item>
    <item>On this day...</item>
    <item>Todos</item>
    <item>Step Count</item>
  </string-array>
</resources>
```

This is how it shows up on the list menus. Go ahead and click on the `Todos` menu item and we'll interact with the items in the following sections:

Next, we will implement a menu for our `Todo` app using the `WearableNavigationDrawer` component from the Android Wear API. The menu will let us choose a different view (tab) corresponding to the type of to-do item (for example, home, work, and so on) and list to-do items of that type when the drawer tab is selected.

About the navigation drawer

Navigation drawer is a material object accessible from a sheet that slides down from the top edge of the screen. A navigation drawer is ideally suited for apps that have multiple views. Pagination dots guide users between views through a left or right swipe.

Navigation drawers offer a feature whereby the content of each view becomes visible when the user scrolls to the top of the view. The drawer stays open for five seconds if idle, after which it is hidden.

Complementing the navigation drawer is an action drawer object that is accessible from a material sheet that slides up from the bottom edge of the screen. Swiping up reveals the action drawer that holds additional actionable content.

The TodosActivity class

Implementing a navigation drawer involves creating a drawer layout using the `WearableDrawerLayout` class and adding to it a view that contains the main content of the screen. This primary view has child views that contain the contents of the drawer. The `TodosActivity` class will control navigation drawers and initialize drawer layouts:

```
public class TodosActivity extends WearableActivity implements
WearableActionDrawer.OnMenuItemClickListener
{
  private static final String TAG = TodosActivity.class.getName();
  private WearableDrawerLayout mWearableDrawerLayout;
  private WearableNavigationDrawer mWearableNavigationDrawer;
  private WearableActionDrawer mWearableActionDrawer;
  private List<TodoItemType> todoItemTypes =
Arrays.asList(TodoItemType.HOME, TodoItemType.WORK);
  private TodoItemType mSelectedTodoItemType;
  private TodoItemTypeFragment mTodoItemTypeFragment;

  @Override
  protected void onCreate(Bundle savedInstanceState)
  {
    super.onCreate(savedInstanceState);
    Log.d(TAG, "onCreate()");
```

```
    setContentView(R.layout.activity_todo_main);
    setAmbientEnabled();

    //defaulted to Home todo item type
    mSelectedTodoItemType = TodoItemType.HOME;

    // Initialize content
    mTodoItemTypeFragment = new TodoItemTypeFragment();
    Bundle args = new Bundle();
    args.putString(TodoItemTypeFragment.ARG_TODO_TYPE,
mSelectedTodoItemType.toString());
    mTodoItemTypeFragment.setArguments(args);
    FragmentManager fragmentManager = getFragmentManager();
    fragmentManager.beginTransaction().replace(R.id.content_frame,
mTodoItemTypeFragment).commit();

    // Main Wearable Drawer Layout that wraps all content
    mWearableDrawerLayout = (WearableDrawerLayout)
findViewById(R.id.drawer_layout);

    //Top Navigation Drawer
    mWearableNavigationDrawer = (WearableNavigationDrawer)
findViewById(R.id.top_navigation_drawer);

    Log.i(TAG, "mWearableNavigationDrawer  = " +
mWearableNavigationDrawer);
    mWearableNavigationDrawer.setAdapter(new  NavigationAdapter(this));

    // Peeks Navigation drawer on the top.
    mWearableDrawerLayout.peekDrawer(Gravity.TOP);

    // Bottom Action Drawer
    mWearableActionDrawer = (WearableActionDrawer)
findViewById(R.id.bottom_action_drawer);
    mWearableActionDrawer.setOnMenuItemClickListener(this);

    // Peeks action drawer on the bottom.
    mWearableDrawerLayout.peekDrawer(Gravity.BOTTOM);
  }
}
```

The TodoItemTypeFragment class

The `TodoItemTypeFragment` class is an inner class of the `TodosActivity` activity and contains content for each type of to-do item. For the sake of simplicity, we show some static content (highlighted in the following code). Refer to `Chapter 5`, *Synchronizing Data,* for information on synchronizing data between wearable and handheld apps:

```
public static class TodoItemTypeFragment extends Fragment
{
  public static final String ARG_TODO_TYPE = "todo_type";
  TextView titleView = null;
  TextView descView = null;
  public TodoItemTypeFragment()
  {
    // Empty constructor required for fragment subclasses
  }
  @Override
  public View onCreateView(LayoutInflater inflater, ViewGroup  container,
Bundle savedInstanceState)
  {
    View rootView = inflater.inflate(R.layout.fragment_todo_item,
container, false);
    titleView = (TextView)  rootView.findViewById(R.id.todo_card_title);
    descView = (TextView)  rootView.findViewById(R.id.todo_card_desc);
    String todoType = getArguments().getString(ARG_TODO_TYPE);
    TodoItemType todoItemType = TodoItemType.valueOf(todoType);
    updateFragment(todoItemType);
    return rootView;
  }
  public void updateFragment(TodoItemType todoItemType)
  {
      titleView.setText(todoItemType.getTypeValue() + " Todos");
      //The following line is hardcoded on purpose for simplicity
      descView.setText("List description");
  }
}
```

This is what the to-do item card will look like. Note that the `Home` to-do item is selected as default, as mentioned in the preceding code sample:

The NavigationAdapter class

Navigation adapter controls what's shown in a navigational state. We implement the `WearableNavigationDrawerAdapter` class to populate the contents of the navigation drawer:

```
private final class NavigationAdapter extends
WearableNavigationDrawer.WearableNavigationDrawerAdapter
{
  private final Context mContext;
  public NavigationAdapter(Context context)
  {
    mContext = context;
  }

  @Override
  public int getCount()
  {
    return todoItemTypes.size();
  }

  @Override
  public void onItemSelected(int position)
  {
    Log.d(TAG, "WearableNavigationDrawerAdapter.onItemSelected():   " +
position);
    mSelectedTodoItemType = todoItemTypes.get(position);
    String selectedTodoImage =  mSelectedTodoItemType.getBackgroundImage();
    int drawableId =  getResources().getIdentifier(selectedTodoImage,
"drawable",  getPackageName());
    mTodoItemTypeFragment.updateFragment(mSelectedTodoItemType);
```

```
    }

    @Override
    public String getItemText(int pos)
    {
      return todoItemTypes.get(pos).getTypeValue();
    }

    @Override
    public Drawable getItemDrawable(int position)
    {
      mSelectedTodoItemType = todoItemTypes.get(position);
      String navigationIcon =  mSelectedTodoItemType.getBackgroundImage()
      int drawableNavigationIconId =
  getResources().getIdentifier(navigationIcon, "drawable",  getPackageName())
      return mContext.getDrawable(drawableNavigationIconId);
    }
}
```

Navigation item

While on the**Home Todos** screen (if you recall, Home was the default type), let's swipe down from the top. As expected, the Home to-do type was pre-selected:

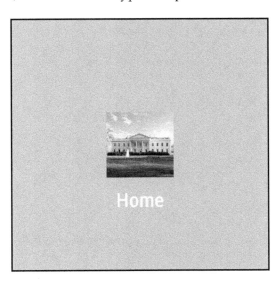

The WearableDrawerLayout class

The `activity_todo_main.xml` file contains the definition of the root drawer layout containing a top navigation drawer and a bottom action drawer. Take note of the menu layout highlighted:

```xml
<android.support.wearable.view.drawer.WearableDrawerLayout
    android:id="@+id/drawer_layout"
    xmlns:android="http://schemas.android.com/apk/res/android"
    xmlns:app="http://schemas.android.com/apk/res-auto"
    xmlns:tools="http://schemas.android.com/tools"
    android:layout_width="match_parent"
    android:layout_height="match_parent"
    android:background="@color/black"
    tools:context=".TodosActivity"
    tools:deviceIds="wear">

    <FrameLayout
        android:layout_width="match_parent"
        android:layout_height="match_parent"
        android:id="@+id/content_frame"/>

<android.support.wearable.view.drawer.WearableNavigationDrawer
    android:id="@+id/top_navigation_drawer"
    android:layout_width="match_parent"
    android:layout_height="match_parent"
    android:background="@color/light_grey" />

<android.support.wearable.view.drawer.WearableActionDrawer
    android:id="@+id/bottom_action_drawer"
    android:layout_width="match_parent"
    android:layout_height="match_parent"
    app:action_menu="@menu/action_todo_drawer_menu"
    android:background="@color/dark_grey"/>

</android.support.wearable.view.drawer.WearableDrawerLayout>
```

Menu items

The `activity_todo_drawer_menu.xml` file contains the definitions of the individual drawers:

```xml
<menu xmlns:android="http://schemas.android.com/apk/res/android">
    <item android:id="@+id/menu_add_todo"
    android:icon="@drawable/ic_add_to_list"
    android:/>
```

```
<item android:id="@+id/menu_update_todo"
android:icon="@drawable/ic_todo_list"
android: />

<item android:id="@+id/menu_clear_todos"

android:icon="@drawable/ic_clear_list"
android: />
</menu>
```

While on the `Home Todos` index card (shown in a previous image), swiping from bottom to the top will show the action drawer:

Menu listener

Clicking on individual menu items, we just display the toast message. Like we said earlier, we want to make the code concise and easily readable. Based on the chapters we covered earlier, we should have an understanding of how to perform data synchronization for these individual menu actions. We have used the `onMenuItemClick` class to perform the menu listener activity, shown as follows:

```
@Override
public boolean onMenuItemClick(MenuItem menuItem)
{
  Log.d(TAG, "onMenuItemClick(): " + menuItem);
  final int itemId = menuItem.getItemId();
  String toastMessage = "";
  switch (itemId)
  {
    case R.id.menu_add_todo:
    toastMessage = "Adding " +  mSelectedTodoItemType.getTypeValue() + "
```

```
Todo";
    break;

    case R.id.menu_update_todo:
    toastMessage = "Updating " +  mSelectedTodoItemType.getTypeValue() + "
Todo";
    break;

    case R.id.menu_clear_todos:
    toastMessage = "Clearing " +  mSelectedTodoItemType.getTypeValue() + "
Todos";
    break;
  }
  mWearableDrawerLayout.closeDrawer(mWearableActionDrawer);
  if (toastMessage.length() > 0)
  {
    Toast toast = Toast.makeText(getApplicationContext(), toastMessage,
Toast.LENGTH_SHORT);
    toast.show();
    return true;
  }
  else
  {
    return false;
  }
}
```

Clicking on the **Add Todo** option performs the following action:

Switching to-do types

Now if we pull the drawer down from the top edge of the screen and swipe from right to left, we switch to a different to-do item as shown in the following image, which in effect displays a new navigation item:

If we pull the drawer back to the top, it has the effect of setting the navigation item to the current selection. This happens using the `onItemSelected` method of the `WearableActionDrawer.OnMenuItemClickListener` class implemented by the `TodosActivity` activity:

```
@Override
public void onItemSelected(int position)
{
   Log.d(TAG, "WearableNavigationDrawerAdapter.onItemSelected(): " +
position);
   mSelectedTodoItemType = todoItemTypes.get(position);
   String selectedTodoImage =  mSelectedTodoItemType.getBackgroundImage();
   int drawableId = getResources().getIdentifier(selectedTodoImage,
"drawable", getPackageName());
   mTodoItemTypeFragment.updateFragment(mSelectedTodoItemType);
}
```

Here is what we see:

Pulling from bottom to top, we see the menu items such as **Add Todo**, **Update Todo List**, and **Clear List** again. Here is what we see when we click on the **Clear List** menu item:

Summary

In this chapter, we obtained an intuitive understanding of what material design really is, and we explored several key principles relevant to Android Wear design and development. We implemented navigation drawers for our `Todo` app that add the ability to switch between to-do types and view the to-do items that perform actions specific to each type.

10
Watch Faces

"If you spend too much time thinking about a thing, you'll never get it done."
– Bruce Lee

We will begin this chapter with an introduction to the concept of watch faces and survey the Android Wear APIs available to help us develop them. We will then develop a simple interactive watch face that, in addition to showing time, responds to a tap action by showing the number of days elapsed in the year and the number remaining.

The code accompanying this chapter is available for reference on GitHub (`https://github.com/siddii/mastering-android-wear/tree/master/Chapter_10`).
For the sake of brevity, code snippets are only included as needed. The reader is encouraged to download the referenced code from GitHub and follow along as they progress through the chapter.

Telling the time

When we speak of wearable devices, we are overwhelmingly referring to smartwatches, and a watch that does not tell the time isn't really much of a watch. It's like having a luxury yacht that features state of the art GPS technology but has trouble staying afloat. To strike a metaphor closer to home, consider a smartphone that has trouble functioning as a phone. (Wait! That's actually happened!)

What is a watch face?

The term *watch face* is used to refer to the digital display of the current time on the wearable device so that the user can tell at a glance what the time is, in much the same way one does when wearing a watch.

Unlike a traditional watch, however, our wearable has a multitude of additional functionalities restricted only by its own internal memory and its communication with one or more paired handheld companion devices. So, showing the time on a wearable speaks to a far more sophisticated piece of software than, say, software that is written for a digital watch that may have a specific list of functionalities–time, date, dual time, and alarm mode to name a few.

Needless to say, the watch face is itself a replaceable component in a wearable. You can change it to one you like, as often as you like. Watch faces sporting an array of styles and shapes, some offering relevant contextual data, are available through the Android Wear companion app. A user simply selects an available watch face, either on the wearable or on the companion app, and the wearable device displays a preview of the watch face and allows the user to configure it. And if you can't find what you like, you can go ahead and write your own. Hence, this chapter. Our journey through implementing a watch face will feel more real when we get to build one in the next section. Let's first touch upon what a watch face design entails, and which Wear API classes come into play in the development of a watch face.

Design considerations

While Android Wear can be a huge help in your design efforts through the provision of various capabilities such as attractive colors, dynamic backgrounds, animations, and data integrations, there are non-API aspects to your design that must be considered. We list a few here that are widely embraced by the Android development community:

- Think about what you want to show the user and how that fits into the context of a watch face. Too much information can distract.
- Your watch face should run reliably on square and circular devices.
- Provide a suitable implementation for the ambient mode. Users will thank you for not draining their wearable's battery life when it is idle.
- UI indicators (such as notification cards) should still show up without making it impossible to read the time.

- Enrich your watch face with intelligence to query and display context-sensitive information available through the companion handheld device. Remember, the companion app does all the heavy lifting, so your wearable app (in this case, your watch face) should delegate to the companion app any computation-intensive work or third-party data lookup, such as weather information.

Let the user configure the watch face.

We highly recommend that you read through the *Watch Faces for Android Wear* section, which will help as a design guide, available on the Android developers site (`https://devel oper.android.com/design/wear/watchfaces.html`).

Implementation considerations

Considering the background images. The background image in interactive mode may be different than the one used in ambient mode. Furthermore, background images should be scaled down (as a one-time operation) if the device has a lower resolution than the image.

Application code that retrieves context-sensitive data should only run on as-needed basis, with results being stored for reuse when the watch face needs to be redrawn.

Updates to the watch face in ambient mode should be as simple as possible through the use of a limited set of colors, a fixed black background, and with only outlines being drawn to minimize work and conserve battery life.

The watch face service

A watch face is implemented as a service and packaged inside a wearable app. You already know that wearable apps are, in turn, packaged inside handheld apps. When users install such a handheld app that contains a wearable app with one or more watch faces, these watch faces then become selectable in the watch face picker on the wearable. They are also available on the handheld device in the Android Wear companion app. When one of the watch faces is selected (either on the handheld or the wearable's picker), the watch face is shown on the wearable device, which invokes the service callback methods as required through the life cycle of the watch face.

To create watch face implementations, we extend the classes provided in the Wearable support library (the `android.support.wearable.watchface` package). When a watch face becomes active, the system invokes the methods in its service class when various events occur, such as a change in time, a switch to ambient mode, and a notification alert. The implementations of the corresponding handlers then respond by drawing the watch face using the updated time or the notification data or whatever other data the event may consume. Key methods that may need to be implemented in a watch face service include following:

- The `onCreate` method
- The `onPropertiesChanged` method
- The `onTimeTick` method
- The `onAmbientModeChanged` method
- The `onDraw` method
- The `onVisibilityChanged` method

Check out the Wearable support library at `https://developer.android.com/reference/android/support/wearable/watchface/package-summary.html` for a close look at the object model of the available watch face service classes.

Once implemented, the watch face service must be registered in the manifest (`AndroidManifest.xml`) file of the wearable app. This is how the system makes the watch face available in both the Android Wear companion app and the watch face picker on the wearable device when a user installs the app.

Interactive watch faces

Watch faces do support limited user interaction. A single tap gesture at a given location on the watch face is accepted as long as it does not conflict with another UI element also listening for that gesture. In our sample code in the next section, we support a tap gesture that shows the number of days elapsed in the current year, as well as the number of days remaining.

Handling tap events involve implementing the `setWatchFaceStyle` method available in all extensions of the `WatchFaceService.Engine` class. The app informs the system that the watch face receives tap events, as shown in the following snippet:

```
setWatchFaceStyle(new WatchFaceStyle.Builder(mService)
  .setAcceptsTapEvents(true)

  // other style customizations
```

```
.build());
```

Performance considerations

Conserving power is quite critical in the context of watch faces because a watch face is always active. Here are a few best practices put forward by the Wear development community with respect to watch face development:

- Ensure that the watch face only performs actions when it is active. Use the `onVisibilityChanged` and `isVisible` methods of the `WatchFaceService.Engine` class to determine that.
- Avoid using the `WearableListenerService` element to listen for events, as it is called whether or not a watch face is active. Rather, use listeners registered with the `DataApi.addListener` element.
- Keep an eye on the actual power consumed by our wearable app. The Android Wear companion app lets us see how much battery different processes on the wearable device consume.
- When using animations, take care to lower the frame rate. 30 frames per second are sufficient for a smooth animation experience. We should use animations as little as possible, and when we do use them, we should use every opportunity to let the CPU sleep between runs of our animation. Every idle cycle contributes to a larger effort at conserving battery life.
- Keep the bitmaps small. Where it makes sense, combine multiple bitmaps into one. Reducing the number of graphic assets we draw contributes to power savings.
- Use the `Engine.onDraw` method exclusive to perform drawing operations. Move any work that loads resources, resizes images, or performs computations external to drawing, out of the `onDraw` method. Consider locating such code in the `onCreate` method instead.

Let's build a watch face

It's time to see the concepts, introduced previously, in action. We will build a simple watch face that shows the time using a fairly standard hour, minutes, and seconds display. Tapping the watch face will show the number of days that have elapsed in the current year. A second tap will show the number of days remaining in the current year.

In the subsections that follow, we will define a `WatchFaceService` class that extends the API `CanvasWatchFaceService` class and overrides the relevant event handlers that pertain to our sample application.

The Android manifest file

We begin by declaring the `TodayWatchFaceService` service and the `WatchFaceConfigActivity` activity, which helps with selecting a background color for the watch:

```
<!-- Required to act as a custom watch face. -->
<uses-permission android:name="android.permission.WAKE_LOCK" />

<service
  android:name=".TodayWatchFaceService"
  android:label="@string/digital_name"
  android:permission="android.permission.BIND_WALLPAPER" >
  <meta-data
    android:name="android.service.wallpaper"
    android:resource="@xml/watch_face" />

  <meta-data
    android:name="com.google.android.wearable.watchface.preview"
    android:resource="@drawable/preview_digital" />

  <meta-data
    android:name="com.google.android.wearable.watchface.preview_circular"
    android:resource="@drawable/preview_digital_circular" />

  <meta-data
android:name="com.google.android.wearable.watchface.companionConfigurationA
ction"
    android:value="com.siddique.androidwear.today.CONFIG_DIGITAL"/>

  <meta-data
android:name="com.google.android.wearable.watchface.wearableConfigurationAc
tion"
    android:value="com.siddique.androidwear.today.CONFIG_DIGITAL"/>
  <intent-filter>
    <action android:name="android.service.wallpaper.WallpaperService" />

    <category
android:name="com.google.android.wearable.watchface.category.WATCH_FACE" />
  </intent-filter>
</service>
```

this

```
<activity
  android:name=".WatchFaceConfigActivity"
  android:label="@string/digital_config_name" >
  <intent-filter>
    <action android:name="com.siddique.androidwear.today.CONFIG_DIGITAL" />

    <category
android:name="com.google.android.wearable.watchface.category.WEARABLE_CONFI
GURATION" />
    <category android:name="android.intent.category.DEFAULT" />
  </intent-filter>
</activity>
```

The TodayWatchFace service

Before we take a closer look at the implementation of the TodayWatchFaceService class,
let's run our sample code to see how it behaves so that we can observe the app from a user
standpoint.

Note that long pressing on the device screen causes the installed watch faces to get
displayed:

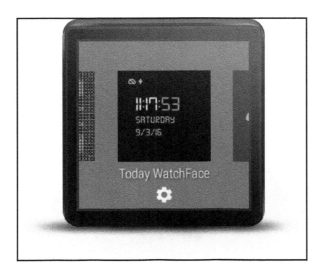

Note that a *gear* icon shows up underneath the label, the `TodayWatchFace` activity, of our custom watch face because we have a configuration activity defined for the `WatchFace` element. Let's select our custom watch face. Here's how it renders. By default, it shows the day of the week and the full date with the *seconds* colon blinking:

Tapping once on the watch face shows the day of the year, as shown in the following image:

Tapping a second time on the watch face shows the number of days left in the year.

Tapping again takes us back to the default display.

The TodayWatchFaceService class

The `TodayWatchFaceService` class does all of the work, including setting the layout, reading the configuration values, and painting the UI for every tick of the second. It isn't realistic to discuss over 700 lines of code in this chapter. So, we'll look at important snippets taken from this class definition:

```
public class TodayWatchFaceService extends CanvasWatchFaceService {
  @Override
  public Engine onCreateEngine()
  {
    return new Engine();
  }
  private class Engine extends CanvasWatchFaceService.Engine  implements
DataApi.DataListener,  GoogleApiClient.ConnectionCallbacks,
GoogleApiClient.OnConnectionFailedListener
  {
    ...
  }
}
```

As always, the sample source code for this chapter, and all others, is available at the GitHub link provided at the beginning of each chapter. The source code hosted at GitHub is our primary reference for a thorough understanding of how this service works.

The onTimeTick method

This method is called for every time tick. We invalidate the UI (see the call to the
`invalidate()` method) to force a call to the `onDraw` method. In effect, we re-render the UI
every 500 milliseconds in normal mode and every minute in ambient or mute mode:

```
@Override
public void onTimeTick()
    {
      super.onTimeTick();
      if (Log.isLoggable(TAG, Log.DEBUG))
      {
        Log.d(TAG, "onTimeTick: ambient = " + isInAmbientMode());
      }
      invalidate();
    }
```

Drawing the watch face

The `onDraw()` method paints the watch face with all necessary information. Follow the
comments in the code to make complete sense of the following code snippet:

```
@Override
public void onDraw(Canvas canvas, Rect bounds)
{
    long now = System.currentTimeMillis();
    mCalendar.setTimeInMillis(now);
    mDate.setTime(now);
    boolean is24Hour =
DateFormat.is24HourFormat(TodayWatchFaceService.this);

    // Show colons for the first half of each second so the colons blink on
when the time
    // updates.
    mShouldDrawColons = (System.currentTimeMillis() % 1000) < 500;

    // Draw the background.
    canvas.drawRect(0, 0, bounds.width(), bounds.height(), mBackgroundPaint);

    // Draw the hours.
    float x = mXOffset;
    String hourString;
    if (is24Hour)
    {
      hourString =
```

```
formatTwoDigitNumber(mCalendar.get(Calendar.HOUR_OF_DAY));     }
  else
  {
    int hour = mCalendar.get(Calendar.HOUR);
    if (hour == 0)
    {
      hour = 12;
    }
    hourString = String.valueOf(hour);
  }
  canvas.drawText(hourString, x, mYOffset, mHourPaint);
  x += mHourPaint.measureText(hourString);

  // In ambient and mute modes, always draw the first colon.  Otherwise,
draw the
  // first colon for the first half of each second.
  if (isInAmbientMode() || mMute || mShouldDrawColons)
  {
    canvas.drawText(COLON_STRING, x, mYOffset, mColonPaint);
  }
  x += mColonWidth;

  // Draw the minutes.
  String minuteString =
formatTwoDigitNumber(mCalendar.get(Calendar.MINUTE));
  canvas.drawText(minuteString, x, mYOffset, mMinutePaint);
  x += mMinutePaint.measureText(minuteString);

  // In unmuted interactive mode, draw a second blinking colon  followed by
the seconds.
  // Otherwise, if we're in 12-hour mode, draw AM/PM
  if (!isInAmbientMode() && !mMute)
  {
    if (mShouldDrawColons)
    {
      canvas.drawText(COLON_STRING, x, mYOffset, mColonPaint);
    }
    x += mColonWidth;
    canvas.drawText(formatTwoDigitNumber(mCalendar.get(Calendar.SECOND)), x,
mYOffset, mSecondPaint);
  }
  else if (!is24Hour)
  {
    x += mColonWidth;
    canvas.drawText(getAmPmString( mCalendar.get(Calendar.AM_PM)), x,
mYOffset, mAmPmPaint);
  }
```

```
    // Only render the day of week and date if there is no peek card, so they
do not bleed
    // into each other in ambient mode.
    if (getPeekCardPosition().isEmpty())
    {
        if (tapCount == 0)
        {
            // Day of week
            canvas.drawText(mDayOfWeekFormat.format(mDate), mXOffset, mYOffset +
mLineHeight, mDatePaint);
            canvas.drawText(mDateFormat.format(mDate), mXOffset, mYOffset +
mLineHeight * 2, mDatePaint);
        }
        else if (tapCount == 1)
        {
            // Day of Year
            canvas.drawText("Day of year", mXOffset, mYOffset + mLineHeight,
mDatePaint);
            canvas.drawText(Integer.toString(TodayUtil.getDayOfYear()), mXOffset,
mYOffset + mLineHeight * 2, mDatePaint);
        }
        else if (tapCount == 2)
        {
            // Days left in Year
            canvas.drawText("Days left in year", mXOffset, mYOffset +
mLineHeight, mDatePaint);
            canvas.drawText(Integer.toString(TodayUtil.getDaysLeftInYear()),
mXOffset, mYOffset + mLineHeight * 2, mDatePaint);
        }
    }
}
```

Ambient mode

Ambient mode, in contrast with interactive mode, is the energy saver mode. Depending on the watch and its configuration, an operation such as a click on a dial renders the watch faces in ambient mode:

It may not be obvious at a glance because our app is so simple, but if we compare the preceding screenshot with the screenshot of the watch face in interactive mode, we will see that the seconds don't show up and the colon symbol doesn't blink.

Here's the listener that gets called when the watch face switches from interactive mode to ambient mode:

```
@Override
public void onAmbientModeChanged(boolean inAmbientMode)
{
  super.onAmbientModeChanged(inAmbientMode);
  if (Log.isLoggable(TAG, Log.DEBUG))
  {
    Log.d(TAG, "onAmbientModeChanged: " + inAmbientMode);
  }
  adjustPaintColorToCurrentMode(mBackgroundPaint,
mInteractiveBackgroundColor,WatchFaceUtil.COLOR_VALUE_DEFAULT_AND_AMBIENT_B
ACKGROUND);
  adjustPaintColorToCurrentMode(mHourPaint,
mInteractiveHourDigitsColor,WatchFaceUtil.COLOR_VALUE_DEFAULT_AND_AMBIENT_H
OUR_DIGITS);
  adjustPaintColorToCurrentMode(mMinutePaint,
mInteractiveMinuteDigitsColor,
WatchFaceUtil.COLOR_VALUE_DEFAULT_AND_AMBIENT_MINUTE_DIGITS);

  // Actually, the seconds are not rendered in the ambient mode, so we
could pass just any
  // value as ambientColor here.
  adjustPaintColorToCurrentMode(mSecondPaint,
mInteractiveSecondDigitsColor,
WatchFaceUtil.COLOR_VALUE_DEFAULT_AND_AMBIENT_SECOND_DIGITS);

  if (mLowBitAmbient)
  {
    boolean antiAlias = !inAmbientMode;
```

```
   mDatePaint.setAntiAlias(antiAlias);
   mHourPaint.setAntiAlias(antiAlias);
   mMinutePaint.setAntiAlias(antiAlias);
   mSecondPaint.setAntiAlias(antiAlias);
   mAmPmPaint.setAntiAlias(antiAlias);
   mColonPaint.setAntiAlias(antiAlias);
  }
  invalidate();
  // Whether the timer should be running depends on whether we're in
ambient mode (as well
  // as whether we're visible), so we may need to start or stop the timer.
  updateTimer();
}
```

Customizing the watch face

We did not want to take this example too far, so in the interest of simplicity, we decided to provide a configurable watch face background color. Clicking on the gear icon from the watch face settings lets us pick the background color, as shown here:

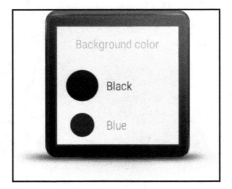

The WatchFaceConfigActivity class

The WatchFaceConfigActivity class renders a simple color picker to determine the background color:

```
public class WatchFaceConfigActivity extends Activity implements
WearableListView.ClickListener, WearableListView.OnScrollListener
{
  @Override
  protected void onCreate(Bundle savedInstanceState)
```

```
    {
        super.onCreate(savedInstanceState);
        setContentView(R.layout.activity_digital_config);
        mHeader = (TextView) findViewById(R.id.header);
        WearableListView listView = (WearableListView)
findViewById(R.id.color_picker);
        BoxInsetLayout content = (BoxInsetLayout) findViewById(R.id.content);
    }
}
```

Here's a screenshot of the watch face when we select a background color of navy blue:

We've just scratched the surface of watch face design and development, but hopefully, the basic treatment here has given us a taste of the work involved and piqued our interest. We could get a lot more creative in displaying relevant contextual information for a given day, such as the number of to-do items, weather-related information, and so on. As with all knowledge acquisition, we see that as we get done, we're really just getting started.

Summary

In this chapter, we introduced the concept of watch faces and looked at their design, implementation, and performance considerations. We then surveyed the `WatchFaceService.Engine` class before implementing a simple interactive watch face and seeing these concepts and API classes in action.

11

Advanced Features and Concepts

"Man is a genius when he is dreaming."
– Akira Kurosawa

In this chapter, we introduce the design concerns and API features related to making apps run as if they were always on. We develop an activity to demonstrate the always-on capability. We then touch upon debugging wear apps over Bluetooth connections and conclude with a preview of Android Wear 2.0.

 The code accompanying this chapter is available for reference on GitHub (`https://github.com/siddii/mastering-android-wear/tree/master/Chapter_11`). Note that for the sake of brevity, code snippets are only included as needed. The reader is encouraged to download the referenced code from GitHub and follow along as they progress through the chapter.

Keeping the watch running

You may recall our discussion of watch faces in the previous chapter wherein a watch face starts out running in interactive mode. As the screen times out, the watch face continues to run as the device goes into its power-saving ambient mode.

While this feature, meaning the watch face's always-on capability, is inherent to watch faces–we don't want our watch to slack off when we want the time–it is not necessarily inherent to all wearable apps. For instance, if we had our `todo` app or `Step counter` app active, it would only be a matter of time before the screen timed out and rendered the watch face. If we then wanted to return to our app, we would have to interact with our wearable device to snap it out of ambient mode and bring up our last used activity or app. We can imagine scenarios where this can be a source of user frustration.

Fortunately, if our devices are running Android version 5.1 or higher, we can harness the power of the Android Wear APIs to conserve power during the execution of our wearable apps. These devices allow apps to remain in the foreground while still conserving battery power. Apps can be coded to control what is displayed in ambient mode even as they continue fulfilling their primary purpose, whatever that may be. Such apps are, in effect, always on.

Making an app to stay always on

Here are some of the things we need to do and/or keep in mind when looking to enable ambient mode for our wearable apps:

- Our SDK should be updated to include the Android 5.1 or higher platform as this version provides activities with ambient mode support. See the *Android SDK Packages* section in `Chapter 2`, *Setting up Development Environment on Android Studio*, for more information.
- We must set our manifest `targetSdkVersion` to API level 22 or higher (that is, version 5.1).
- We may choose to provide backward compatibility for devices running an Android version prior to 5.1 by specifying a `minSdkVersion` attribute. By doing so, the activities that support ambient mode will automatically fall back by returning to the home screen and exit the activity.
- Our activities should extend the `WearableActivity` API class so as to inherit all the methods needed to enable ambient mode.
- We should invoke the `setAmbientEnabled()` method in the`onCreate()` listener of our activity.
- We should have a clear understanding of the transitions between interactive and ambient mode and the relevant listeners that are called during those transitions, as shown in the figure at the end of this section.

- We should pay special attention to updating the activity UI in the ambient mode to use a basic layout and a minimal palette of colors to maximize better power conservation.
- We should try to update the activity UI using a consistent layout so that the transition between interactive and ambient modes appears as seamless as possible to the user.
- We should exercise care not to update the screen too frequently when in ambient mode. Remember that the whole point of the ambient mode is to save power. Updating the activity UI more frequently than 10 seconds can be a source of power drainage and be counter-productive to enabling ambient mode altogether. If it does become necessary to perform more frequent updates due to the nature of the app (as with mapping or fitness), consider the use of the API's `AlarmManager` class (`https://developer.android.com/reference/android/app/AlarmManager.html`).

 It is worth repeating that devices running a version of Android prior to 5.1 (API Level 22) may not have access to the always-on capabilities of the newer APIs, but they should still run these apps without errors provided we specify a `minSdkVersion` attribute of 20 or higher in the manifest.

Consider the following diagram, depicting the update in the UI activity of the screen:

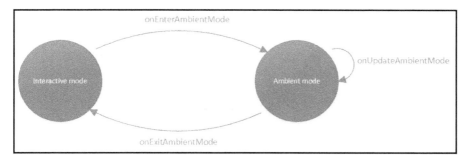

An always running step counter

Now, let's demonstrate everything we presented in the previous section in practice by augmenting our step counter from `Chapter 7`, *Voice Interactions, Sensors, and Tracking*, to be always on. Let's dive right in.

The Android manifest file

The first thing to do is to update the `AndroidManifest.xml` file and set up the `StepCounterActivity` class to have its `launchMode` set to `singleInstance`. This is necessary in order to update the screen more than once per minute in ambient mode. Not doing so will cause the `AlarmManager` class to launch an intent to open a new activity every time the alarm is triggered rather than reusing the same (already active) activity. Here is the snippet from the file:

```
<activity
    android:name=".StepCounterActivity"
    android:label="@string/daily_step_count_title"
    android:launchMode="singleInstance"
/>
```

As soon as we launch our step counter, we see a colorful background image and a display showing the number of steps taken so far since a reboot of the device, as shown in the following screenshot:

The StepCounterActivity class

This activity does the bulk of the work for our step counter. We modify the `onCreate()` method with a call to the `setAmbientEnabled()` method setting it to true. We also define a helper method, `refreshDisplayAndSetNextUpdate()`, that we call from our `onCreate()` listener, as well as the `onEnterAmbient()` and `onUpdateAmbient()` listeners. A call to the `isAmbient()` method determines whether we use the value from the ambient interval or the active interval. Furthermore, in ambient mode, we remove the background, make the pixels black, and paint the data with a white foreground. Maximizing the use of black and minimizing the use of white directly contributes to battery power conservation.

The following code listing presents the StepCounterActivity class for our step counter:

```
public class StepCounterActivity extends WearableActivity  implements
SensorEventListener
{
  private SensorManager mSensorManager;
  private Sensor mSensor;

  // Steps counted since the last reboot
  private int mSteps = 0;

  private static final String TAG =  StepCounterActivity.class.getName();
  private BoxInsetLayout stepCounterLayout;
  private CardFrame cardFrame;
  private TextView title, desc;
  private AlarmManager mAmbientStateAlarmManager;
  private PendingIntent mAmbientStatePendingIntent;

  /**
   * This custom handler is used for updates in "Active" mode. We use a
separate static class to
   * help us avoid memory leaks.
   */

  private final Handler mActiveModeUpdateHandler = new UpdateHandler(this);

  /**
   * Custom 'what' for Message sent to Handler.
   */

  private static final int MSG_UPDATE_SCREEN = 0;

  /**
   * Milliseconds between updates based on state.
   */

  private static final long ACTIVE_INTERVAL_MS =
TimeUnit.SECONDS.toMillis(1);
  private static final long AMBIENT_INTERVAL_MS =
TimeUnit.SECONDS.toMillis(20);

  @Override
  protected void onCreate(Bundle savedInstanceState)
  {
```

```
    super.onCreate(savedInstanceState);
    setContentView(R.layout.activity_daily_step_counter);

    mSensorManager = (SensorManager)
getSystemService(Context.SENSOR_SERVICE);
    mSensor = mSensorManager.getDefaultSensor(Sensor.TYPE_STEP_COUNTER);

    setAmbientEnabled();

    mAmbientStateAlarmManager = (AlarmManager)
getSystemService(Context.ALARM_SERVICE);
    Intent ambientStateIntent = new  Intent(getApplicationContext(),
DailyTotalActivity.class);

    mAmbientStatePendingIntent = PendingIntent.getActivity(
      getApplicationContext(),
      0 /* requestCode */,
      ambientStateIntent,
      PendingIntent.FLAG_UPDATE_CURRENT);

    stepCounterLayout = (BoxInsetLayout)
findViewById(R.id.step_counter_layout);
    cardFrame = (CardFrame)  findViewById(R.id.step_counter_card_frame);
    title = (TextView) findViewById(R.id.daily_step_count_title);
    desc = (TextView) findViewById(R.id.daily_step_count_desc);
    refreshDisplayAndSetNextUpdate();
  }

  /**
   * Loads data/updates screen (via method), but most importantly, sets up
the next refresh
   * (active mode = Handler and ambient mode = Alarm).
   */

  private void refreshDisplayAndSetNextUpdate()
  {
    Log.i(TAG, "Refresh display and set next update ");
    refreshStepCount();
    long timeMs = System.currentTimeMillis();
    if (isAmbient())
    {
      /** Calculate next trigger time (based on state). */
      long delayMs = AMBIENT_INTERVAL_MS - (timeMs %  AMBIENT_INTERVAL_MS);
      long triggerTimeMs = timeMs + delayMs;

      /**
       * Note: Make sure you have set activity launchMode to singleInstance
in the manifest.
```

```
       * Otherwise, it is easy for the AlarmManager launch intent to open a
new activity
       * every time the Alarm is triggered rather than reusing this
Activity
       */

      mAmbientStateAlarmManager.setExact(
        AlarmManager.RTC_WAKEUP,
        triggerTimeMs,
        mAmbientStatePendingIntent);

    }
    else
    {
      /** Calculate next trigger time (based on state). */
      long delayMs = ACTIVE_INTERVAL_MS - (timeMs %  ACTIVE_INTERVAL_MS);

      mActiveModeUpdateHandler.removeMessages(MSG_UPDATE_SCREEN);
      mActiveModeUpdateHandler.sendEmptyMessageDelayed  (MSG_UPDATE_SCREEN,
delayMs);
    }
  }

  /**
   * Prepares UI for Ambient view.
   */

  @Override
  public void onEnterAmbient(Bundle ambientDetails)
  {
    Log.d(TAG, "onEnterAmbient()");
    super.onEnterAmbient(ambientDetails);

    /** Clears Handler queue (only needed for updates in active mode). */

    mActiveModeUpdateHandler.removeMessages(MSG_UPDATE_SCREEN);

    /**
     * Following best practices outlined in WatchFaces API (keeping most
pixels black,
     * avoiding large blocks of white pixels, using only black and white,
     * and disabling anti-aliasing, etc.)
     */

    stepCounterLayout.setBackgroundColor(Color.BLACK);
    cardFrame.setBackgroundColor(Color.BLACK);
    desc.setTextColor(Color.WHITE);
    desc.getPaint().setAntiAlias(false);
```

```
        title.setTextColor(Color.WHITE);
        title.getPaint().setAntiAlias(false);
        refreshDisplayAndSetNextUpdate();
    }

    @Override
public void onUpdateAmbient()
{
        Log.d(TAG, "onUpdateAmbient()");
        super.onUpdateAmbient();

        refreshDisplayAndSetNextUpdate();
}

/**
 * Prepares UI for Active view (non-Ambient).
 */
@Override
public void onExitAmbient()
{
        Log.d(TAG, "onExitAmbient()");
        super.onExitAmbient();

        /** Clears out Alarms since they are only used in ambient mode. */
        mAmbientStateAlarmManager.cancel(mAmbientStatePendingIntent);

        stepCounterLayout.setBackgroundResource(R.drawable.jogging);
        cardFrame.setBackgroundColor(Color.WHITE);

        desc.setTextColor(Color.BLACK);
        desc.getPaint().setAntiAlias(true);

        title.setTextColor(Color.BLACK);
        title.getPaint().setAntiAlias(true);

        refreshDisplayAndSetNextUpdate();
    }
}
```

As a result of the preceding changes, this is how the step counter shows up in ambient mode now:

Debugging wearable apps

An important and extremely useful tool available to developers is the ability to set up debugging for our wearable apps running on our wearable device. We have the ability to run debug commands from our development machine to troubleshoot our wearable apps and have any debug output from the wearable be sent over to the handheld, which in turn must be connected to the development machine. Some setup is required in order to accomplish this. The general connectivity between devices is as shown in the following diagram:

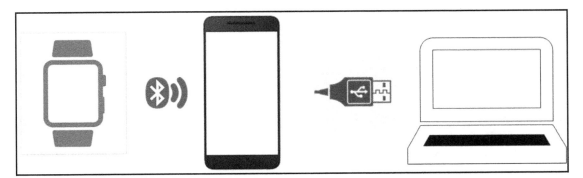

The greatest payoff here is that we don't need to run two separate USB connections from the development machine–one to the handheld and the other to the wearable device. Instead, we can deploy and debug code straight to the handheld device from the development machine using a Bluetooth connection. This becomes especially helpful when such troubleshooting needs to be performed repetitively during development. Without this feature, we would have to endure the clutter of too many cables, and we know we can do without that.

Device setup

Debugging must be set up on the companion handheld as well as the wearable device, albeit a bit differently.

USB debugging on the handheld app

Follow the steps mentioned to perform the debugging on the handheld app:

1. Launch the **Settings** screen in the handheld device and make sure the USB debugging is turned on in **Developer options**.
2. Locate and launch the **Developer options**. Alternatively, you may have to tap the **About Phone** menu, scroll down the build number and tap it seven times to activate the **Developer Options** menu item. Tap it once it is available.
3. Choose to enable **USB debugging**, as shown in the following screenshot:

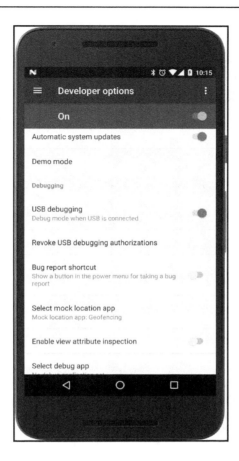

Bluetooth debugging on the wearable app

Follow the steps mentioned here to perform debugging on the wearable app using Bluetooth:

1. Launch the **Wear** menu by tapping the home screen twice.
2. Launch **Settings**.
3. Locate and launch **Developer Options**. Alternatively, you may have to tap **About Phone**, scroll down the build number and tap it seven times to activate the **Developer Options** menu item. Tap it once it is available.
4. Choose to enable **Debugging over Bluetooth** option.

Session setup on the handhelds apps

Perform the following steps to set up the session in handheld apps:

1. Launch the Android Wear companion app on the handheld.
2. Launch **Settings** from the menu in the top-right corner:

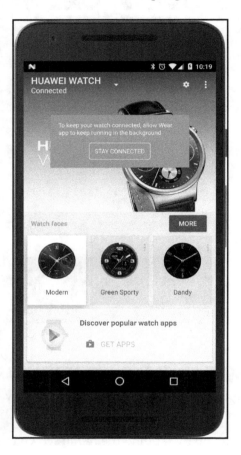

3. Choose to enable the **Debugging over Bluetooth** option. Note that the following message shows up on your handheld under that option:

```
Host: disconnected
Target: connected
```

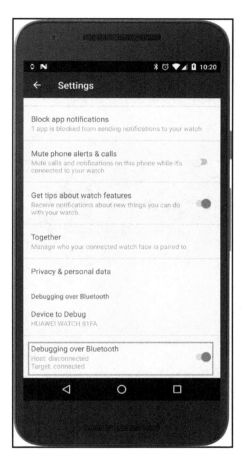

This is because we are yet to connect your handheld to your development machine. Let's do that next.

Let's now connect the handheld to our development machine using a USB cable, and type the following at the `adb` command prompt. We use an arbitrary port `4444`, we could use any available port:

```
adb forward tcp:4444 localabstract:/adb-hub
adb connect localhost:4444
```

In the companion app on the handheld, you should now see the following under the **Debugging over Bluetooth** option:

```
Host: connected
Target: connected
```

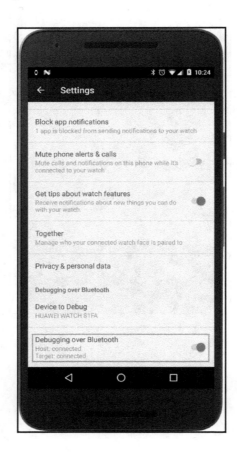

We have thus completed setting up a debugging session for our wearable. After the successful connection, we see a notification shown as follows on the wearable device:

Now, let's test it all out by executing some debug commands.

Note that if we execute the `adb devices` command at the `adb` command prompt, we should see our wearable device show up as `localhost:4444`. We can now execute the `adb` commands to debug our application, using the following format:

```
adb -s localhost:4444 <command>
```

Consider following command, for example:

```
adb -s localhost:4444 shell
```

In the developer options in the wearable device, we can see that the **ADB debugging** and **Debug over Bluetooth** options are enabled:

Now that we have established a successful connection between the development machine, handheld device and wearable device, we will be able to deploy and debug our code straight from Android Studio to the wearable device using the Bluetooth connection. The watch will show up as a deployment target, depicted in the following screenshot:

The way forward – reviewing Android Wear 2.0

Back when we began work on this book, Android Wear 2.0 was well past ideation and into design. The Android Wear preview API was still in the works, being scheduled for release about the time we rounded a corner taking us past the halfway point of our first draft. Although the 2.0 APIs are still being fleshed out and development is underway, interested developers can try it out as part of the Android Wear 2.0 developer preview edition of the API.

In this section, we are going to highlight some of the key new features being baked into the 2.0 APIs, with an eye on what we've seen in the previous chapters of this book.

Watch face complications

In our discussion of watch faces, we had advanced the idea of interactive watch faces whereby we made available limited user interaction with the watch face primarily through tap gestures. Android Wear 2.0 formalizes such additional display complexity into the idea of a complication. A complication is essentially any feature that displays data beyond the time, that is, the hours and minutes. Version 2.0 offers a watch face complications API that lets watch faces display extra information without requiring underlying plumbing to get the data. Instead, the provision of data–be it a battery level indicator, or weather information–is externalized through the complications API to a complication data provider, which then takes control of how the data is rendered on the watch face. The watch face that consumes data from such a complication data provider is still responsible for drawing the complications.

Navigation and action drawers

Android Wear 2.0 API is heavily based on material design from top to bottom, and we see the realization of its design principles in the core components and stock widgets.

We introduced the navigation and action drawers back in Chapter 9, *Material Design*, in the course of a discussion on material design. Android Wear 2.0 has further solidified the alignment of these widgets with material design concepts.

There is additional support for drawer peeking so that users may access these drawers as they scroll. Also, the peek view and navigation drawer closure operations have been automated with the added ability to show the first action in the `WearableActionDrawer` API's peek view. These drawer widgets are also extensible in the new 2.0 APIs with support to create custom drawers.

Expanded and messaging style notifications

Android Wear 2.0 has made significant changes to notifications and the visual interactions with them. Users can get an improved experience through what are called expanded notifications. When we specify additional content pages and actions for a notification, they become available to the user in an expanded notification. Each expanded notification follows material design principles. The user can view the expanded notification by simply tapping on a notification. However, the notification would have to be generated by an app on the paired companion handheld, and it should not have a `Notification.contentIntent` class set for it.

The 2.0 version also offers a `Notification.MessagingStyle` class, which uses chat messages included in a `MessagingStyle` notification. The result is an enhanced app-like experience in the expanded notification.

The Input Method Framework

Android's **Input Method Framework (IMF)** allows users to enter text using the system's default IME or third-party IMEs. The input may be accomplished through tapping individual keys or by gesture typing. Android Wear 2.0 extends these same capabilities to wearable devices. Users will have the ability to enable more than one IME from a list of installed IMEs with one of them set as the default.

Remote input and smart reply

Wear 2.0 allows users to choose from a range of input options through the remote input API. These include dictation, emoji, smart reply, a developer-provided list of canned response, and the default IME.

In addition, developers can enable a *smart reply* feature for their notifications whereby users get a fast and reliable means to respond to chat messages. Contextually-relevant choices can be made to appear in expanded notifications, as well as in remote input.

Wrist gestures

Imagine being able to interact with our wearable device through a mere flick of our wrist. That is exactly what the designers of the Wear 2.0 APIs had in mind when they provided for the enablement of two wrist gestures for use by apps–the *Flick Wrist Out* and the *Flick Wrist In* gestures. A typical use case for this would be scrolling through a list of notifications or news articles while doing anything that forces you to interact with one hand only, for instance, when there is a large cup of coffee in the other hand.

Wrist gestures in 2.0 can be enabled/disabled by going to **Settings** | **Gestures** | **Wrist Gestures**.

Bridging mode

Notifications are, by default, shared (also known as bridged) from an app on a companion handheld to wearable device. If there is also a standalone wearable app issuing the same notifications, then this can be a source of annoyance, as the same notification appears from the standalone app as well as from the companion handheld, owing to the bridging.

To ameliorate this issue, the Android Wear 2.0 Preview edition includes a feature called **bridging mode**. This mode allows the standalone app to turn on or off, through its manifest, the bridging of notifications from the companion handheld app. Further, the APIs permit notification dismissals to be synchronized across devices through the declaration of dismissal IDs.

Standalone wearables

This was inevitable. The companion handheld is a valuable design metaphor in making the apps smart with respect to resource usage. But with perpetual strides in concentrating power and memory into small-form devices, the possibility of reducing dependence on companion handhelds, or even doing away with them, is becoming more and more real.

Standalone devices will let wearable apps work independently of companion apps. Rather than having an Android Wear app be embedded in its corresponding companion app (as is currently the case), the use of multi-APK delivery method will allow developers to release Android Wear apps independently of their corresponding companion apps.

APK is the Android file format used for installation to the Android operating system. We'll talk more about this in the next chapter. For now, suffice it to understand that Google Play offers multi-APK support that lets us publish different APKs for our apps, each targeting a different device configuration. Thus, each APK is an independent version of the app, even though they may share the same application listing and package name on Google Play. Each APK is also signed with the same release key.

Eliminating dependence on the companion app, in turn, eliminates the need for a wearable data layer API. Android Wear apps will be able to make network requests directly. Furthermore, direct access to network resources opens up new ways for Wear apps to authenticate. These ways include the following:

- Using the standard Google keyboard for direct text entry
- Using the `android.accounts.AccountManager` API class to sync and store account data

Summary

We began this chapter with a discussion of how to keep our apps running when our wearable device goes into ambient mode. We then augmented our step counter activity using our `Today` app from `Chapter 7`, *Voice Interaction, Sensors, and Tracking*, to make it always on, thereby getting up close to the parts of the Android Wear API that let us enable ambient mode for our apps. We then concluded with a brief note on debugging wearable apps over Bluetooth before proving a sneak preview of Android Wear 2.0.

12
Publishing Apps to Google Play

"I always believe that the sky is the beginning of the limit."
- MC Hammer

Testing is an important precursor to the distribution of the app via Google Play store. In this chapter, we will provide an overview of the importance of testing our Android Wear app and the tooling available for it, as well as how to automate UI testing. We will conclude the chapter with step-by-step instructions on how to get the app ready for publishing.

Testing

It does not take too long for any programmer to learn the hard and valuable lesson that testing code is as important as coding itself. Ignore that lesson and a QA team worth its salt will be sure to bring you to your knees. Testing all on its own is a topic that deserves a lot of attention. There are countless resources, including books, out there that will sell you on a wide array of testing methodologies and philosophies. **Test-driven Development (TDD)** is worth researching if you are new to testing.

However, all that is out of the scope of this book. In this chapter, we are more concerned about the testing tooling provided by the Android platform geared toward Wear development, as well as the test APIs that are at your disposal. Let's take a closer look at that in the sections that follow.

The need for testing

The single most compelling reason to test code, in general, is to catch regressions as early as possible in the application development life cycle. With every code change that is made, there is a possibility that it has impacted the way another area of the system works, often negatively. But by crafting well thought out (repeatable) tests for every isolated and smallest possible unit of code, we have a means to ensure that it continues to function as it is meant to. These unit tests are critical validation points that, through their failures, raise flags of code instability.

Since each piece of code is to be tested in isolation, it often becomes necessary to simulate the forces that are external to the unit of code in question. Mocking frameworks used in conjunction with unit tests make this easy; for example, mocking an external service that is called by the unit under test.

Types of unit test

Based on whether the unit of code runs independent of the Android platform, there are two types of tests, local tests and instrumented test:

- **Local tests**: These tests are the unit tests that run on the local **Java Virtual Machine (JVM)**. Any code run as a local test will run without any dependency on the Android system, or it will at the very least be able to simulate such a dependency through a mocking framework.
    - The online documentation for the step-by-step instruction on unit tests can found at `https://developer.android.com/training/testing/unit-testing/index.html`.
- **Instrumented tests**: These tests, in contrast, run on an Android device or emulator and are the recommended approach to run unit tests that have Android dependencies that are too complex or involved to simulate using mocking frameworks. These tests provide ready access to instrumentation information, such as access to the global information about an application environment through the `android.content.Context` class.

    - For step-by-step instructions on building instrumented tests, refer to the documentation at `https://developer.android.com/training/testing/unit-testing/instrumented-unit-tests.html`.

One difference that will jump out at you right away is that in your Android Studio project, the source files for local unit tests are stored in the `module-name/src/test/java` folder, while the source files for instrumented unit tests are stored in the `module-name/src/androidTest/java` folder.

Automating user interface tests

For Wear apps in particular, there are certain aspects of development that need to be tested very carefully, and unit tests may not be sufficient in these cases. Complex UI interactions are one such example. Ideally, a human tester would be able to catch many of these issues, but it does not take long for that to prove inefficient in terms of time and cost, not to mention prone to human error and oversight.

By writing our UI tests to simulate human interaction, we can save time and increase confidence in the quality of our tests. Automated UI tests are coded in the same designated Android test folder as our instrumented unit tests, that is, the `module-name/src/androidTest/java` folder.

Code implemented in this folder is built by the Android plugin for Gradle and executed on the same device that the app is intended to run on. This lets us use UI testing frameworks to simulate user interactions on the target app. Furthermore, automated UI tests may span a single app or multiple apps.

Single app tests, using a UI testing framework such as **Espresso**, allow us to programmatically simulate user interactions such as entering a specific input on a specific activity. They also let us exercise the effects of user interactions on various activities of the app by letting us test that the correct UI output is rendered in response to a piece of user interaction.

Multi-app tests (also known as the cross-app functional tests), using a UI testing framework such as UI Automator, let us verify interactions between apps. For instance, if we wanted our test to launch (say) the calculator app and perform a calculation that will, in turn, be used to drive an input to a field in our app, **UI Automator** makes this possible.

Test APIs

Android tests are based on **JUnit**. We write our unit or integration test classes as JUnit 4 classes.

JUnit

JUnit is an instance of the **xUnit** architecture for unit testing frameworks. It offers a way to perform common setup, teardown, and assertion operations in our unit tests. A test class can contain one or more methods. Common JUnit annotations can be used to mark a method that performs setup work (the `@Before` class) or teardown work (the `@After` class) work. The `@Test` annotation marks a test method.

From within a JUnit test class, we can use the `AndroidJUnitRunner` test runner class to invoke the Espresso or UI Automator APIs to implement our user interactions and inter-app simulations.

The AndroidJUnitRunner class

The `AndroidJUnitRunner` class is a test runner that lets us run JUnit test classes on Android devices. The test runner loads our test package and our app to a device and then runs our tests and reports results. Apart from JUnit support, the `AndroidJUnitRunner` class includes the following features:

- **Access to instrumentation information**: An `InstrumentationRegistry` class provides easy access to the instrumentation object, the target app's `Context` object, and the test app's `Context` object. This data becomes particularly useful when our tests use the UI Automator framework.
- **Test filtering**: In addition to standard annotations supported by JUnit 4, some Android-specific annotations are also available. The `@RequiresDevice` annotation specifies that the test should run only on physical devices (and not on emulators). The `@SdkSuppress` annotation keeps the test from running on an Android API level that is lower than a specified level; for example, the `@SDKSupress(minSdkVersion=18)` annotation will suppress tests on all API levels that are lower than 18.
- **Test Sharding**: The `AndroidJUnitRunner` class provides support to split a test suite into multiple shards thereby allowing the grouping of tests by any given shard (identifiable by an index number).

Espresso

Espresso is a testing framework geared toward testing user flows within an app. It provides a set of APIs that let us craft tests that use the implementation details from the app that is being tested. Features include view and adapter matching, action APIs, and UI thread synchronization, each discussed briefly in the following sections.

View and Adapter matching

The `Expresso.onView()` method gives us access to a specific UI component in the target app. The method searches the view hierarchy for a match and returns a View reference that meets the specified criteria (which is supplied as part of the matcher argument passed to the method). Consider the following example:

```
onView(withId(R.id.my_button));
```

The returned reference can then be used to perform user actions on it or test assertions against it.

While View matching lets you bring back a View reference, Adapter matching is useful when the target View is inside a layout that is subclassed from the `AdapterView` class. In this case, only a subset of the layout's views may be loaded in the current view hierarchy. The `Espresso.onData()` method can be used to access a target view element.

Action APIs

Using the `android.support.test.espresso.action.ViewActions` API, we can perform user actions such as clicks, swipes, button presses, text entry, and hyperlinking.

UI Automator

Google's UI Automator provides a set of APIs that enables UI tests to interact with user apps and system apps. The UI Automator API lets us programmatically open the **Settings** menu or the app launcher on a test device. If the test code does not depend on the implementation details of the target app, then the UI Automator framework can be a good candidate for writing automated tests.

This framework includes the following components:

- The UI Automator viewer to inspect layout hierarchy and view properties of UI components that are visible in the device foreground. This tool is located in the `<android-sdk>/tools` directory.
- The `android.support.test.uiautomator.UiDevice` API to retrieve state information and perform operations on the device on which the target app is running. The `UiDevice` class supports operations such as changing the device rotation, pressing the back, home, or menu buttons; and taking a screenshot of the current view.

The following code snippet demonstrates how the `UiDevice` class can be used easily to simulate a short press on the home button:

```
mDevice = UiDevice.getInstance(getInstrumentation());
mDevice.pressHome();
```

- The UI Automator APIs that support cross-app UI testing. These APIs let us capture and manipulate UI components across multiple apps.

Monkey and monkeyrunner

Monkey is a command-line tool that sends pseudorandom streams of gestures, keystrokes and touches to devices. It is run via the **Android Debug Bridge** (**ADB**) tool, and is primarily meant to stress test your app.

Monkeyrunner is an API and execution environment for test programmers coded in Python. It includes functions for connecting to a device, installing and uninstalling packages, taking screenshots, and so on. A monkeyrunner command-line tool is available to run programs that use the monkeyrunner API.

For a more in-depth look at these topics, as well as how to measure UI performance and automate UI performance tests, we should take a look at the online documentation on the developer's site (`https://developer.android.com/training/testing/start/index.htm l`) as our primary reference.

The human touch

No matter how solid our automated testing strategy, we really haven't tested our app until we have used it. That is why it is paramount to set time aside in our development cycle to test out the various features of our app, as well as user interactions. Every UI implementation code path must be exercised. There is no substitute for visual verification when it comes to confirming that our screens render acceptably in both square and round watch faces.

There may also be valuable insights gained to help us improve the way our user interactions are implemented. We should leverage the material design concepts we covered in previous chapters and use them to our advantage as much as possible.

App distribution

In the previous section, we covered in some detail how to test our app. Testing is a prerequisite for distribution, and it would serve us well to familiarize ourselves with what differentiates a Wear app in terms of quality. Check out the article from the online documentation at `https://developer.android.com/distribute/essentials/quality/wear.html`, which serves as a reminder in this regard.

Once we have implemented our well-designed app and tested it as much as we can, we can start preparing to distribute it to potential users. That is the focus of this section to examine how to ready and distribute our Wear apps to users through Google Play.

Packaging

As we go through the process of building our release APKs using Android Studio, we find that two different APKs are generated, one for mobile and one for wearable.

Packaging a wearable app in Android Studio involves the following steps:

1. Replicate all permissions from the manifest file of the wearable app module to the manifest file of the handheld app module.
2. Ensure that the wearable and handheld app modules have the same package name and version number.
3. Specify a Gradle dependency in the handheld app's `build.gradle` file to the wearable app module.
4. Navigate to **Build | Generate Signed APK...**.

These steps are illustrated in the following screenshot:

Pick a module to generate the APK for mobile or wear, as shown in the following screenshot:

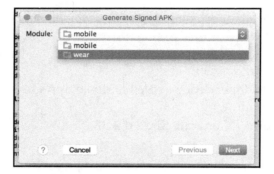

Specify your release keystore by creating a new one or picking the one you already have available:

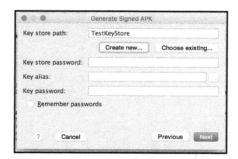

Here, we create a new keystore path and sign our app using it:

Specify a destination folder for the APK files and then click **Finish**, as shown in the following screenshot:

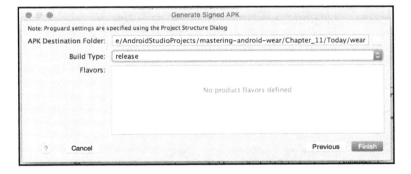

We should now find the two APK files available in the folder we specified:

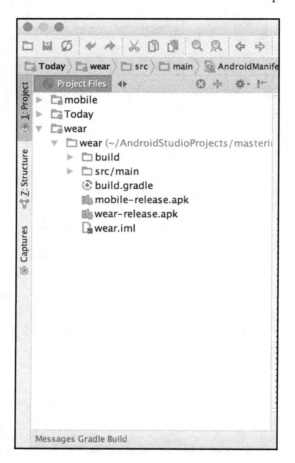

Publishing and opt-in

Once we have built our APKs, run it through our tests for Wear app quality and determined that it is ready for release, we upload it to the **Developer Console**. This is the step during which we set up distribution options and update the store listing with any screenshots of our Wear app. A detailed launch checklist is available in the online documentation (https ://developer.android.com/distribute/tools/launch-checklist.html), and it is recommended that you read it prior to publishing.

Once our app is ready for release, we may opt into Android Wear from the *Pricing and Distribution* section of the Developer Console. Opt-in implies that our app meets the Wear app quality criteria and is an affirmation that we want our app to be made more discoverable to Android Wear users through Google Play. Consider the following diagram depicting the process:

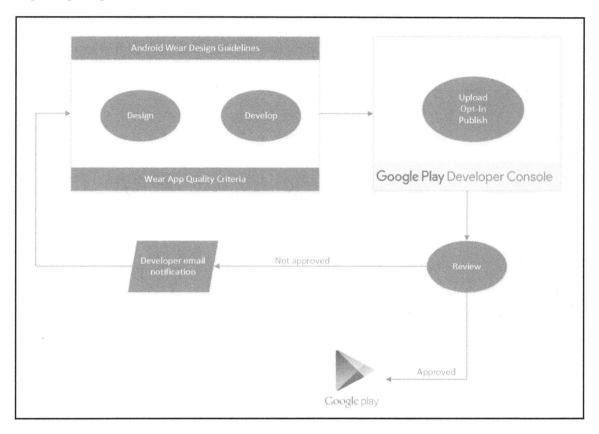

Once we have opted in, we can publish our app as usual, at which stage Google Play submits our app for review against the **Wear App Quality criteria**. We are notified of the results once they become available. If the app is found to meet all the Wear App quality criteria, Google Play will proceed to make it more discoverable to Android Wear users.

If, however, the app is found to fall short, then an e-mail notification is sent to our developer account address with the areas highlighted requiring our attention. Once we address these issues, we can upload a new version of our app to the Developer Console to initiate another round of opt-in and review.

The *Pricing and Distribution* page in the *Android Wear* section of the **Google Play Developer Console** holds the review and approval status of our app at any given time.

We click on the **Add new application** button, as shown in the following screenshot, to upload our app:

We specify a default language and a title before proceeding to upload the APK:

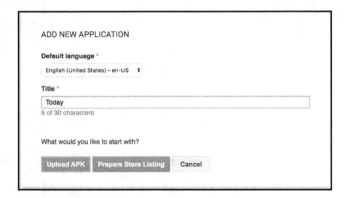

Choose the type of release, that is, **Production**, **Beta**, or **Alpha Testing** , and then click the relevant **Upload** button:

We then pick our Wear (or mobile) APK file and attempt the upload, depicted in the following screenshot:

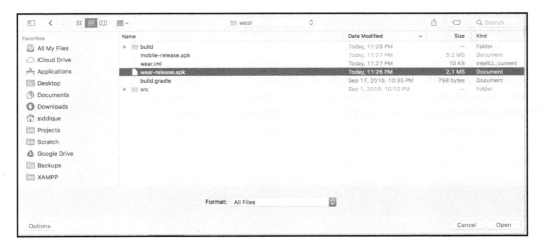

At this point, we are prompted to fill in app metadata that is necessary for publishing:

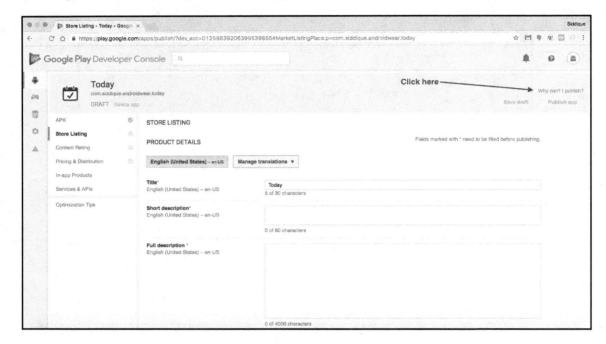

We can click on the **Why can't I publish?** link in the top-right corner to display any items that are missing. Here is an example of all the items needed to publish the app. Once they are added, the app should be ready for publishing:

WHY CAN'T I PUBLISH?

You need to complete the points below before you can publish your application.

You need to add a high-res icon. [English (United States) – en-US]
You need to add a feature graphic. [English (United States) – en-US]
You need to add at least 2 non-Android TV screenshots. [English (United States) – en-US]
You need to select a category.
You need to select a content rating.
You need to add a short description. [English (United States) – en-US]
You need to add a full description. [English (United States) – en-US]
You need to acknowledge that this application meets the Content Guidelines.
You need to acknowledge that this application complies with US export laws.
You need to target at least one country.
You need to enter a privacy policy URL.
You need to make your application free or set a price for it.
You need to declare whether or not your application contains ads.
Your app is missing a required content rating. Go to your app's Content Rating page and complete a rating questionnaire.

Close

Summary

In this chapter, we introduced Android testing and distinguished between local unit tests and instrumented tests. We then summarized the tooling available for testing our wear apps in Android Studio before we took a brief look at how to accomplish automation with UI testing. We concluded with a discussion of the stages that must be traversed when preparing our apps for distribution via Google Play.

Index

Delivery 95
NotificationCompat.Builder 94, 95
wearable-only actions 95

D

DayOfYearActivity activity
about 57
activity_day_of_year.xml file 58, 60

E

Espresso
about 193, 194
adapter matching 195
view matching 195

F

FakeGPS application
reference 96
used, for mocking locations 107

G

Geofencing API
about 96
reference 96
Git
about 17
reference 17
GitHub
about 17
reference 17
GPS
mocking 96
Gradle build files 34
Gradle
about 17
reference 18
gyroscope 123

H

handheld app
about 121, 122
session, setting up on 182, 183, 184, 185, 186
USB debugging, performing on 180
Human Computer Interaction (HCI) 142

I

Input Method Framework (IMF) 188
instrumented tests
about 192
reference 192
Integrated Development Environment (IDE) 15
IntelliJ IDEA platform 15
interactive watch faces 158

J

Java Virtual Machine (JVM) 192
JSoup library
reference 80
JUnit 194

L

local tests 192
locations
mocking, FakeGPS used 107

M

main activity layout file 53, 54
material design
about 143
approaching 139, 140
interaction, with world 140, 141, 142
Monkey 196
monkeyrunner 196
Moore's Law 9
motion sensors
about 122
accelerometer 124
gyroscope 123
reference 123

N

navigation drawer 145
Near Field Communications (NFC) 10
notifications API
core classes 94
Nymi
reference 11

www.ingramcontent.com/pod-product-compliance
Lightning Source LLC
LaVergne TN
LVHW081340050326
832903LV00024B/1237